FINITE PROGRAMMING IN C++

FINITE PROGRAMMING IN C++

Michael T. Wen

iUniverse, Inc.
New York Lincoln Shanghai

FINITE PROGRAMMING IN C++

iUniverse books may be ordered through booksellers or by contacting:

iUniverse
2021 Pine Lake Road, Suite 100
Lincoln, NE 68512
www.iuniverse.com
1-800-Authors (1-800-288-4677)

ISBN-13: 978-0-595-35189-3 (pbk)
ISBN-13: 978-0-595-79885-8 (ebk)
ISBN-10: 0-595-35189-1 (pbk)
ISBN-10: 0-595-79885-3 (ebk)

Printed in the United States of America

Contents

Preface

When I was about to graduate from the University of Santa Barbara with a bachelor degree in computer science, I began to wonder what I could do for newcomers in this discipline. As a programmer, I feel an urgent need for them to be aware of the traps and obstacles that I experienced before so that hopefully they could avoid them. I did not feel this exigency until a friend of mine had to write a program involving advanced data structures in a class he took. That program drained more than twenty hours of his time, and worse, he did not get it done on time. Anyone can imagine how frustrated and anxious he was—frustrated at his deficiency in programming and anxious to have it work. What I got out of this experience is that the time one puts in writing a program is definitely not proportional to the finished portion of the program. This fact implies that writing the same program, one person may get it done within two hours and another may have to spend more than ten hours. I realized that programming is not something time can solve; skills and experience play a much bigger role. With years of experience in programming, I decided to write a book that hopefully would benefit newcomers in this field. I have devised a programming model that has helped me finish each and every programming assignment on time, and if it works for me, it works for you. I always do more than I am asked to because I know from the bottom of my heart that only *by doing more can one improve faster*. The stuff I will be discussing with you guys comes from years of experience in programming and any programmer will possibly, if not definitely, benefit from it. This book is intended for intermediate C++ programmers because you need to be familiar with general terminology and concepts of programming. The ultimate goal is that after reading this book, you will be able to program efficiently and *finitely*.

Introduction

Let's face it. Our programming instructors usually care about only whether our programs do what they are supposed to do; we just need to follow some rough guidelines. As long as you can finish them on time and they do what they should do, you are in good shape. In the real world this is also the case. Your clients do not care about how you make the software; as long as the software meets their requirements, you are home safe. That said, this book is not a tutorial; rather, it teaches you how to write programs in an efficient manner, hence the title of this book, "Finite Programming in C++". First of all, you must understand that only the person willing to spend time to learn can make progress. Therefore, if you are determined to be a great programmer, read through every single chapter and work through every single example and make sure you *completely* understand them and maybe through experimentation come up with your own arguments to counter a point I make. Don't just take for granted everything I say; experiment on your own and see for yourself. Make sure you understand the fundamentals of C/C++ and have at least some programming experience before reading this book. As a last note, I would like to state that programming is a work of art, and as such it can never be covered completely by any books or resources. Creativity is what makes programming unique. I can only point you in a direction, and it is you who will be solving problems you encounter in your programming career. It is my belief that after reading the book, you will be able to start programming efficiently and enjoyably.

What This Book Covers

First the book alerts readers to different aspects of C++, including programming conventions, common misconceptions, and tips and pitfalls involving the use of a class and a function. Then it covers a mini-tutorial on highly useful tools that C++ standard libraries provide, including the Standard Template Library and the string class, to make sure programmers are equipped with them. The following chapters are the jewels of the book—how to program efficiently and *finitely*. The next big section is to have readers brush their programming teeth by working through a series of exercises. Below is a list of short descriptions of what each chapter covers:

Chapter 1—why naming conventions are important and how adopting one can avoid potential bugs

Chapter 2—general misconceptions in programming

Chapter 3—traps and tips involving the use of a class

Chapter 4—traps and tips involving the use of a function

Chapter 5—introduction of bugs and how to debug efficiently

Chapter 6—differences between arrays and pointers and how to dynamically allocate memory

Chapter 7—how to use the Standard Template Library

Chapter 8—how to use C++ string class

Chapter 9—introduction of segmentation fault and how to avoid it

Chapter 10—layout of a typical program

Chapter 11—characteristics of a good program and the 4-step model of writing a good program

Chapter 12—characteristics of a good function and the 4-step model of writing a good function

Chapter 13—importance of documentation

Chapter 14—a collection of debugging exercises

Chapter 15—a collection of programming exercises

Chapter 16—a list of big traps and tips

Appendix A—C++ keywords so that readers will be careful not to use them for any other purpose

Appendix B—operator precedence so that readers know the order of evaluations in an expression

Appendix C—useful functions that perform common tasks such as showing the running time of a program and tokenizing a string

Appendix D—a list of small traps and tips

Appendix E—online resources for readers' reference

Final Word—my final word of advice to readers

References—the references I used in writing this book

Terminology and Symbols

First I want you to be familiar with the terminology and symbols I will be using throughout the book. There could exist more than one term that refer to the same thing, and I do my best in using the most common and accepted terms. The following table lists terms, their meanings, and examples. In the example column, sometimes I use ~ to replace the corresponding term for brevity.

Term	Meaning	Example
char	A variable of type char	The function returns a char.
character array	The traditional C string, which is type char[]	This function returns a character array.
char array	Same as above	This function returns a char array.
bool	A variable of type bool	The function returns a bool.
bool array	An array of type bool	The function returns a bool array.
int	A variable of type int	The first argument to getGPA() is an int.
int array	An array of type int	The function returns an int array.
double	A variable of type double	The function returns a double.
double array	An array of type double	The function returns a double array.
string	An instance of C++ string class	The function returns a string.
the invoking object	The object that invokes the function	Student mike; mike.getID(); mike is ~.
struct	A user-defined structure	The name of the struct is foo.
object	An instance of a class	Jennifer is an object of class Students.

The following table lists symbols, their meanings, and examples.

Symbol	Meaning	Example
()	A function	Let's write a function swap() that swaps two elements in an array.
' '	A character	You need to append a '#' to the end of the string.
" "	A string or a word	"inner#beauty#counts#" is a valid input. The word "template" means...
<>	A library header	You need <iostream> in this program.

The following table lists words in different fonts, each of which has a special meaning.

Sample Word	Meaning
./prog_exe 20 100 Go go Jesse.	I use this font to indicate program outputs, user inputs, and actual program code.
data.txt double my_weight get_score() class Students	I put in bold type file names, data types, variable names, instance names, function names, class names, and any other program elements.
Why not let bygones be bygones, Kitty?	I use italic type to indicate emphasis, a special term, and chapter jokes.
Chapter 14 Code Size Figure 15.1	I underline a chapter name, a section name, and a figure.

Very often I use the term "object" to mean "object reference". In the following declarations:

```
Paint circle;
Paint square;
```

where **Paint** is a class, I refer to **circle** and **square** as objects of **Paint** to avoid wordiness. Technically, they are known as object references or instances. Just keep it in mind.

Also, when I explain something, I usually struggle over the way I call the subject person. If I call the person "he", girls may feel a little discriminated against, but if I call the person "she", guys won't be happy. Anyway, I got to choose one, and I choose "he" because it is shorter. Please excuse me for any inconvenience this may cause.

In fact, if you are a girl and are really bothered by it, let me know and if enough people have brought up this request, I promise I will revamp this book and publish the updated version as soon as possible. You have my word.

CHAPTER 1

Naming Conventions

Abeen entered The Month Bank and walked toward a teller, Bushy, to open a savings account.

"So when do you want your account activated?"

"Well, let's see, January, February, March, April, May, June, July—July it is!"

"My God, dude, you count the months exactly the way I do! I always have to start from the first month and reach a destination month one by one."

"Wow, you actually are not used to the way Unistatians name their months?"

"Of course not, man. All 12 months have different names, and they expect me to remember them all? I much prefer naming them Firstmonth, Secondmonth, Thirdmonth ... they would be so much easier to remember."

"Yeah, I am all for that wonderful idea!"

"Okay, now I am going to the Gray House and submit the legislation immediately. Thank you for supporting this idea which has been mocked by all my acquaintances ever since I came up with it..."

So you see, from now on Unistatians have easy-to-remember names for the twelve months, thanks to naming conventions.

1.1   Introduction

Naming conventions are simply conventions in naming elements in a program such as variables, classes, and objects. On the surface, they may seem trivial and arbitrary because technically, one can name them whatever he wants to as long as he doesn't violate the naming rules or use the keywords. However, as you write programs on a regular basis, you will realize that many of the common errors arise from confusion with naming. For example, you may name a class **SystemManager** and one of its objects **systemManager**, but in the program you mistakenly write **SystemManager** when you really mean **systemManager,** or vice versa. Obviously this is a simple syntax error and takes no time to fix, but better naming conventions greatly decrease one's confusion and make names consistent with one another. Therefore it is worthwhile to come up with your own naming conventions and stick to them for the rest of your programming career.

1.2 My Conventions in Naming

By convention, constant variables are all uppercase letters and local variables are a mix of lowercase letters, uppercase letters, and underscores. Personally, I like this convention because it creates distinctions among different contexts of variables. On the other hand, how should we name a variable that means a combination of several things? For example, we may want to name a variable that keeps track of the number of ballots. We can name it **numberofballots**. To shorten it, we name it **numofbal**. Well, this seems fine, but to me a better name is **numOfBal** because we can make it as a rule that each uppercase letter means the start of a new logical word. Under this convention we can easily decrypt a variable's meaning. Some might argue that the name can also be **NumOfBal**, but my convention is that names of objects start with a lowercase letter, and those of a class start with an uppercase letter. Some people like to use underscores as separators, but they can quickly lengthen a name. On the other hand, names of constants are composed of all uppercase letters. Therefore underscores can be used in this case. For example, to name a constant integer that keeps track of ballots, one can do **NUM_OF_BAL**, or simply **NUM_BAL**. In fact, if the program you are writing is a small one and you need to keep track of only one number, then calling it **NUM** is enough.

I have seen programmers use the prefix letter of a variable to indicate its data type. For example, **sName** refers to a string. This convention comes in handy when the same information needs to be represented in several different ways. For example, **sName** is a string and **caName** is a character array. On the other hand, many use the prefix letter to indicate a variable's context. For example, prefix **m** indicates that it's a member variable of a class or a struct; **c** means that it's an instance to a class; **g** means it's a global variable. You get the idea.

In any case, choose your own convention and stick to it for the rest of your programming life. A programmer following his rules long enough usually can remember the names of all variables, classes, objects, and other program elements, and he does not need to go back and forth to remind himself of the name of a certain variable, thereby increasing efficiency and decreasing confusion.

On the other hand, let's say I need 4 **int** to keep track of the ISBNs of four books, I would give them these names: **isbn, isbn2, isbn3, isbn4**. The reason that the first variable does not have a number appended to it is that I usually do not know how many such variables I need. I name it without appending '1' to it and if later I need more variables of the same nature, I begin appending numbers for distinction. An alternative is to use an **int** array.

1.3 Why Name It?

Sometimes naming a variable is not necessary; you can just put everything into a big expression. For example, to convert Fahrenheit to Celsius, you need to subtract 32 degrees from the Fahrenheit temperature, multiply the result by 5, and then divide the result by 9. If you want to write a program that accepts a Fahrenheit temperature from the user then outputs the corresponding Celsius temperature, you can write the following in **main()**:

```
double celsius, fahrenheit;
cout << "Please enter a Fahrenheit temperature: ";
cin >> fahrenheit;
celsius = (fahrenheit-32)*5/9;
cout << "Peter, the corresponding Celsius temperature is " << celsius << endl;
```

However, you also can do:

```
double fahrenheit;
cout << "Please enter a Fahrenheit temperature: ";
cin >> fahrenheit;
cout << "Peter, the corresponding Celsius temperature is " << (fahrenheit - 32)*5/9 << endl;
```

This simple example illustrates an important point: Whenever you think you need to create a variable, think twice. Essentially, the questions you need to ask yourself are:

- Will you use the variable just once or over and over again?
- Will the use of the variable greatly enhance your program's readability (i.e. no magic numbers)?
- Will the use of the variable decrease the running time of your program?

If you need to use the result of an expression many times, you may want to store it in a variable. If the use of the variable can greatly increase your program's readability, it's a good idea to use it. In the above example, a person seeing your program probably understands immediately what the program does if you create a variable called **celsius**. A person unfamiliar with the conversion between Celsius and Fahrenheit may not know what (**fahrenheit** - **32**)***5/9** means. This is just a small example, but in a much larger program, you may need to deal with much more expressions. Then you will make a decision whether or not you should create a variable for each expression. Lastly, you need to know if the use of the variable decreases the running time of your program. Consider the following program:

```
#include <iostream>
using namespace std;
#include <ctime>  /* or <time.h> */
#include <cmath> /* or <math.h> */

int main(int argc, char **argv) {
    int i, i2, i3;
    clock_t start;
    double num, sq;

    cout << "Please enter a positive number: ";
    cin >> num;
    start = clock();
    for(i=0; i<sqrt(num); i++)
        for(i2=0; i2<sqrt(num); i2++)
            for(i3=0; i3<sqrt(num); i3++)
                ;

    cout << "Total is " << (float)(clock() - start) / CLOCKS_PER_SEC << "
    seconds\n";
}
```

As you can see, the program uses the expression **sqrt(num)** in the **for** loops. After several sample runs with **num** being 10000, the average time it takes is about 1.268 seconds on my machine. However, as you can see, we can just calculate it once and store the result in a variable. Here is a version that stores the result of **sqrt(num)** in a variable and uses it whenever the program needs it.

```cpp
#include <iostream>
using namespace std;
#include <ctime>  /* or <time.h> */
#include <cmath> /* or <math.h> */

int main(int argc, char **argv) {
    int i, i2, i3;
    clock_t start;
    double num, sq;

    cout << "Please enter a positive number: ";
    cin >> num;
    sq = sqrt(num);
    start = clock();
    for(i=0; i<sq; i++)
        for(i2=0; i2<sq; i2++)
            for(i3=0; i3<sq; i3++)
                ;
    cout << "total is " << (float)(clock() - start) / CLOCKS_PER_SEC << "
    seconds\n";
}
```

This version runs 0.026 seconds on average on my machine, a dramatic improvement. We all know that the square root of a value takes relatively long time to calculate, so it is a good idea to do such computations once. Again, this is a rather
small example. In a program the result of an expression may need to be computed
many times, given different values in the expression. In any case, whenever you
want to use a variable, think about these questions before you make your move.

If you seize a bat and put it on the ground, it won't be able to fly anymore. They need
to climb to a high spot, then fall into flight.

CHAPTER 2

Misconceptions

Father is scolding Daughter for putting excessive amounts of detergent into the washing machine.
"You idiot! Look at what you have done with the clothes."
"I just want my clothes to be cleaner so that people won't laugh at me."
"You should've consulted me first. You ever tried using gasoline to clean your clothes?"
Father rubbed some gasoline onto a black spot on his shirt, and the spot disappeared shortly.
"See? You shouldn't have put too much detergent. You should've tried gasoline instead."
So they poured one gallon of gasoline into the washing machine and set it to run. In a brief moment the washing machine exploded, burning down their house to ashes.

They say ignorance is human's biggest enemy, now they are talking.

2.1   The More Objects, the Better?

If there are two ways that serve the same purpose and one uses one object and the other uses ten, which way would you prefer? Let's not go into memory management and other technical issues and focus on the efficiency of using one object versus many objects. For example, suppose we need to keep track of however many points on a 2-D space a user enters. He may enter 10, 100, or even 1000 as the number of points. Programmer A writes a class that represents a point and declares as many objects as the user enters. Programmer B writes a class that encapsulates all points and declares only one object that stores all points. Programmer B could obtain many advantages over programmer A, such as neater organization of code, smaller code size, easier manipulation of data, higher efficiency, and less confusion.

That said, how does programmer B manage to use only one object to store everything? He can simply use pointers as data members of the class and allocate space for them dynamically via **new** or **malloc**(). Experienced programmers should have no problem seeing that a big number of objects can be confusing and awkward

7

and the manipulation of which presents pitfalls for making logic errors. Therefore, stay controlled in the number of objects you use in a program.

2.2   The More Functions, the Better?

In general, there are two categories of functions: those belonging to a class, or *member functions*, and those independent of everything, or *nonmember functions*. A function inside a class generally supplements that class by providing operations to manipulate its data members. The main purpose of using a function is that when a module, usually **main**(), wants to do the same task more than once, it can simply call the function that performs the task whenever it needs to. Therefore, it is generally advisable to write functions that help **main**() or any other function do its work, rather than cram everything inside the module.

My experience suggests that in general there should be no more than fifty lines in a function, a hundred tops. This way each function, accompanied by detailed comments, can be understood quickly. Of course too many functions may lead to confusion regarding the passing of function arguments, especially when the arguments contain pointers. That's why we must find a balance between them.

Whenever you want to write a function, carefully think about how often it's needed. Later on in Chapter 4 we will discuss the generality of a function, which is very important for a programmer to fully grasp when a function is necessary and how the function should be written.

2.3   The More Source Files, the Better?

A common conception is that breaking a program into several source files makes the program more modular and thus better. While this may not be a misconception, my experience suggests otherwise. If I have only several small classes inside my program, I put all of them in the file where **main**() resides, along with other necessary helper functions. If I have many big classes, however, I may put them in separate files. In any case, there doesn't exist a rigid rule saying things should be done absolutely one way. Sometimes splitting a program into several files is a good idea; sometimes it isn't. You become more experienced as you program more often.

2.4   Global Versus Local

The main difference between a global variable and a local variable is that a global variable can be accessed anywhere in the program, while a local variable is visible only inside the module it resides. You may be under the impression that using local variables is a lot safer than using global ones, but you miss out on many advantages. In fact, using a global variable, be it an integer or an object of a class, has a big advantage over using a local variable: Every function can access that variable or object. This approach may be advantageous when many functions need access to certain variables. Using global variables may have its insecure aspects, but as long as you know what you are doing, it can hardly cause any trouble. We will see many examples in Chapter 15 regarding how using global variables greatly simplifies program flow and control.

A snail can sleep up to 3 years without ever waking up.

CHAPTER 3

Class

See and Plus are very close buddies. One day they gather together and while they are talking, See abruptly puts his hands over Plus's thing.
"What the hell do you think you are doing?"
"Gosh, calm down, man. Hey, we are friends. We are allowed to touch each other's private parts. See, even husbands and wives sometimes are not close spiritually, but they touch each other, okay?"
"Hm…guess you are right."

So they start touching each other's private parts. What can I say? When C++ was created, friends were allowed to access each other's private members just the same way.

3.1   Private Versus Public Data Members

I am under the impression that instructors who teach beginner programming courses usually encourage the use of private data members because that way, data are directly accessible in only the class' member functions, thereby making data access secure. However, having written so many programs, this is not the impression I have. I usually prefer public variables inside a class because simply using the dot notation allows access to a data item of its objects. You do not need to write a function called **getWhatever**() to get data, nor do you need to write a function called **setWhatever**() to modify data. As for security issues, they are seldom a problem. As long as you know what you are doing, you are unlikely to modify an object's data mistakenly. Therefore, I tend to set the data items of a class to be public. On the other hand, if you want to be absolutely sure that an object is not modified since its declaration, you can make the object **const**, as we will discuss in the next section.

3.2   Const Object and Const Member Functions

Assume **Student** is a class that takes the student's name as an argument in its constructor and **getName()** returns a string which is the name of the student. Let's see how we can promise the compiler that the object will not be modified. Consider the following code snippet:

```
const Student saint = Student("Charlotte Mak");
saint.getName();
```

The object, **saint**, is declared to be **const**, meaning that its data members are not supposed to be altered in any way. However, the member function, **getName()**, needs to guarantee that it won't modify the invoking object. The way to achieve it is to add keyword **const** after the function parentheses. Here is what the **getName()** declaration inside **Student** should look like:

```
string getName() const;
```

Similarly, the function definition, if defined outside **Student**, looks like this:

```
string Student::getName() const {
    return name;
}
```

3.3   Friends

The sole goal of having friends is to allow direct access to private data items of a class object. Friends come in two forms: friend classes and friend functions.

Let's first discuss friend classes. Inside a class, you can declare other classes to be its friends. Doing so allows those classes to access its private members directly. Here is a sample program illustrating this concept:

```
#include <iostream>
using namespace std;

class student {
friend class teacher;  /* now teacher is a friend of student's */
private:
```

```
        int id;
        double gpa;
        char *name;
public:
        student() {
            id = 0;
            gpa = 3.0;
            name = "null";
        }
        int getid() { return id; }
        double getgpa() { return gpa; }
        char* getname() { return name; }
        void changeid(int newid) { id = newid; }
        void changegpa(double newgpa) { gpa = newgpa; }
        void changename(char *newname) { name = newname; }
};

class teacher {
private:
        student *students;
        int size;
public:
        teacher(int num) {
            students = new student[num];
            size = num;
        }
        void renewid();
        void changegpa(int id, double newgpa);
        double getgpa(int id);
};

void teacher::renewid() {
        int i;
        for(i=0; i<size; i++)
            students[i].id = i;  /* accessing student's private data */
}

void teacher::changegpa(int id, double newgpa) {
        int i;
        for(i=0; i<size; i++) {
```

```
            if(students[i].id == id) {  /* accessing student's private data: id */
                students[i].gpa = newgpa;  /* accessing student's private data */
                return;
            }
        }
    }

double teacher::getgpa(int id) {
    int i;
    for(i=0; i<size; i++)
        if(students[i].id == id)  /* accessing student's private data: id */
            return students[i].gpa;  /* accessing student's private data */
    return -1;
}

int main(){
    int i;
    teacher amr(100);

    for(i=0; i<100; i++)
        amr.renewid();
    amr.changegpa(50, 3.99);
    cout << "ID#50 has " << amr.getgpa(50) << " GPA.\n";
    return 0;
}
```

Here is the program's output:

ID#50 has 3.5 GPA.

As we can see, without declaring **teacher** to be a friend of **student**'s, you are not allowed to use the dot notation to access **student**'s private members. You can comment out the first line inside **student** and see what happens when you compile. An alternative to being able to use the dot notation to access **student**'s private members is to simply declare its data members to be public.

After we see how friend classes work, let's now see how friend functions work. Here is a sample program using this feature:

```
#include <iostream>
```

```cpp
using namespace std;

class student {
friend int main();  /* main() is a friend of student's */
friend void showgpa(student s);  /* showgpa() is another friend */
private:
    int id;
    double gpa;
    char *name;
public:
    student() {
        id = 0;
        gpa = 3.0;
        name = "null";
    }
    int getid() { return id; }
    double getgpa() { return gpa; }
    char* getname() { return name; }
    void changeid(int newid) { id = newid; }
    void changegpa(double newgpa) { gpa = newgpa; }
    void changename(char *newname) { name = newname; }
};

void showgpa(student s) {
/* accessing student's private data: name, gpa */
    cout << "The gpa of " << s.name << " is " << s.gpa << ".\n";
}

int main() {
    student mike, john;

    mike.id = 101;
    mike.gpa = 3.91;
    mike.name = "Michael Wen";
/* accessing student's private data: id, gpa */
    cout << mike.name << "'s id is " << mike.id << " and gpa is " <<
mike.gpa
        << ".\n";
    john.id = 102;
    john.gpa = 3.95;
```

```
john.name = "John Wang";
showgpa(john);

return 0;
}
```

As we can see, both **showgpa**() and **main**() can access the private members of **student** by using the dot notation. To make a function a friend to a class, you need to give the name, the return type, and the parameter types of the function, as the example shows. If you comment out the first two lines inside **student** and recompile, the compiler will complain.

To sum up, a friend function or a class has the same access privileges as a member function of the class it is friends with.

3.4 Generic Class

The main purpose of a generic class is to provide genericity so that the same member function does not need to be rewritten to accept a different type. Different programming languages support genericity in different ways. In C++, a class template is used to provide genericity for a class. The word "template" in C++ in fact is linked to genericity. The Standard Template Library we will be covering in Chapter 7 is a case in point. Most of you should be well familiar with a template class; if you don't, consult the Internet or a book for its syntax. Here is a sample program using a template to represent a two-dimensional array:

```
#include <iostream>
using namespace std;

/* you can replace <class Type> with <typename Type> */
template <class Type>
class matrix{
private:
    Type **array;
    int rows;
    int cols;
public:
    matrix(int r, int c);
    matrix(matrix & m);  /* copy constructor */
```

```cpp
        Type* & operator[](int row) { return array[row]; }
        int getRows() const { return rows; }
        int getCols() const { return cols; }
        void showArray();
};

template <class Type>
matrix<Type>::matrix(int r, int c) {
    rows = r;
    cols = c;
    array = new Type*[r];
        for(int i=0; i<r; i++)
            array[i] = new Type[c];
}

template <class Type>
matrix<Type>::matrix(matrix & m) {
    int i, j;
    delete [] array;
    rows = m.getRows();
    cols = m.getCols();
    array = new Type*[rows];
    for(i=0; i<rows; i++)
        array[i] = new Type[cols];
    for(i=0; i<rows; i++)
        for(j=0; j<cols; j++)
            array[i][j] = m[i][j];
}

template <class Type>
void matrix<Type>::showArray() {
    int i, j;
    for(i=0; i<rows; i++) {
        for(j=0; j<cols; j++)
            cout << array[i][j] << '\t';
        cout << endl;
    }
}

int main(){
```

```
int i, j;
matrix<int> b(10,5); /* 10-by-5 array */
matrix<char> d(10,5);

for(i=0; i<10; i++)
      for(j=0; j<5; j++)
            b[i][j] = i+j; /* assigning values to every single cell */
cout << "Here are the contents of b:\n";
b.showArray(); /* display the array */
matrix<int> a(b); /* copy b to a */
cout << "\nHere are the contents of a:\n";
a.showArray();

for(i=0; i<10; i++)
      for(j=0; j<5; j++)
            d[i][j] = 'a'+i+j; /* assigning values to every single cell */
cout << "Here are the contents of d:\n";
d.showArray(); /* display the array */
matrix<char> c(d); /* copy d to c */
cout << "\nHere are the contents of c:\n";
c.showArray();

      return 0;
}
```

Go ahead and add additional functions to this class template so that it can handle row and column additions and deletions. Pay attention to the syntax of a class template and discern the differences between a class template and a normal class.

The primary use of a class template is, obviously, to accommodate a number of different data types. In most situations, however, a class is designed specifically to work with certain data types. Therefore, don't get intimidated by a class template; it is not as important as you may think.

3.5   Traps and Tips

- C++ automatically provides the following member functions for a class: a default constructor, a copy constructor, a default destructor, an assignment operator, and an address operator. Therefore, you can use them without defining them.

- If you do not define any constructor, you can use the default constructor in instantiating a class because compiler automatically creates it for you. If, however, you define a constructor with a set of arguments, then the compiler will not create a default constructor for you. You need to define it explicitly if you want to use it.

- If you want to create an array of objects of a class, the class must have a default constructor.

- A class is almost exactly the same as a struct. You can define constructors, member functions, and so on, inside a struct just like a class. The only difference I can see is that the default context of data members of a class is private and that of a struct is public.

One year is actually 365.242199 days; that's why we have leap years.

CHAPTER 4

Function

Daniel and Sharon were having a fight over an electronic calculator.
"You airhead! How can you use a calculator without putting in batteries?"
"How would I know? I thought pushing the On/Off button was all it needed."
"I can't believe you don't know putting in batteries is the precondition for the calcula-
tor to function."
"Okay, okay, there won't be a next time."
So you see, preserving preconditions is important to make a function work.

There are two types of functions: *member* functions and *nonmember* functions.
Member functions refer to the functions that are associated with a class and nonmember functions are defined as independent modules. In this chapter when I
say function I refer to either type of function unless otherwise specified.

4.1   Preconditions and Postconditions

A function's precondition refers to what must hold before the function is exe-
cuted, and a function's postcondition refers to what will be true or changed after
the execution of the function in addition to what it returns. Knowing exactly the
state of the program before and after the execution of a function is extremely
important. It will greatly reduce logic errors and confusion. From my experience,
many bugs that occur in a program are due to imprecise or incomplete understanding of preconditions and postconditions of one or more functions used in
the program. We will discuss how important they are in Chapter 12.

4.2   One Function Versus More Functions

In my junior year I wrote a program to allow chatting over the Internet between
two or more computer users. In order to make everything work, I wrote many
functions. The total program length is over one thousand lines. When I was
debugging, I needed to scroll up and down to get to the places I wanted.

Therefore, I decided to shrink the code down by combining multiple functions into one. To my embarrassment, I found several functions that were essentially doing the same thing. I combined them and reduced the code size dramatically. The point is that when one function works, why write two or more? Fewer functions also make it easier to debug. On the other hand, when you really need many functions to make the program work, you can do this trick: keep **main()** in one file and all other functions in another. Here is an example.

```cpp
/* "tr.cpp": where main resides */
#include <iostream>
#include <string>
#include "tr.h"
using namespace std;

int main() {
    dummy a;
    dummy2 b;
    dummy3 c;

    a.changeA(1);
    a.changeB('a');
    a.changeC("joy");
    b.a = 2;
    b.b = 'b';
    b.c = "dennis";
    c.a = 3;
    c.b = 'c';
    c.c = "ethan";
    cout << a.getA() << ' ' << a.getB() << ' ' << a.getC() << endl;
    cout << b.a << ' ' << b.b << ' ' << b.c << endl;
    cout << c.a << ' ' << c.b << ' ' << c.c << endl;
    great();
    return 0;
}


/* "tr.h": where all classes and functions reside */
#include <iostream>
#include <string>
using namespace std;
```

```
class dummy{
private:
    int a;
    char b;
    string c;
public:
    dummy() {a=0; b='a'; c="abcde"; };
    int getA() {return a;}
    char getB() {return b;}
    string getC() {return c;}
    void changeA(int val) {a=val;}
    void changeB(char val) {b=val;}
    void changeC(string val) {c=val;}
};

struct dummy2{
    int a;
    char b;
    string c;
};

class dummy3{
public:
    int a;
    char b;
    string c;
};

void great(){
    cout << "Jeremy is diligent and devoted to his parents." << endl;
}
```

After you compile and run it ("g++ tr.cpp –o tr" on my machine), you will see the following output:

```
1 a joy
2 b dennis
3 c ethan
Jeremy is diligent and devoted to his parents.
```

Sometimes separating **main**() from other external classes or functions allows us to debug more easily. You can separate things in as many files as you want; just remember to include appropriate header files in **main**() file, as done in the above example. Also, because **tr.h** uses functions that <iostream> and <string> provide, it needs to include them in the header.

4.3   Recursive Function Versus Non-recursive Function

First of all, let's see the differences between a recursive function and a non-recursive one. A recursive function in general has an extremely high time complexity while a non-recursive one does not. A recursive function generally has smaller code size whereas a non-recursive one is larger. In some situations, only a recursive function can perform a specific task, but in other situations, both a recursive function and a non-recursive one can do it. Here is a recursive version of calculating the Fibonacci number:

```
/* compute n'th Fibonacci number by using recursion */
int fibonacci(int n){
      if(n<=2)
            return 1;
      else
            return fibonacci(n-1) + fibonacci(n-2);
}
```

An experienced programmer should have no problem understanding the logic behind the code. As we can see, in order to compute a Fibonacci number, **Fn**, the function needs to call **Fn-1** and **Fn-2**. **Fn-1** recursively calls **Fn-2** and **Fn-3**, and **Fn-2** calls **Fn-3** and **Fn-4**. In a nutshell, each call recursively computes two values needed to get the result until control hits the base case, which happens when **n<=2**. You can write a simple **main**() that accepts an integer **n** as input and outputs the **n**'th Fibonacci by calling this recursive function and see for yourself how slowly it computes as **n** gets bigger. It gets horrendously slow once **n** gets past 40 on my machine.

Here is a non-recursive version that calculates the Fibonacci number:

```
/* compute n'th Fibonacci number by using a loop */
int fibonacci(int n){
      if(n<=2)
```

```
        return 1;
    int i, last, nextToLast, result;
    last = 1;
    nextToLast = 1;
    result = 1;
    for(i=3; i<=n; i++){
        result = last + nextToLast;
        nextToLast = last;
        last = result;
    }
    return result;
}
```

The logic here is to keep the values already computed in variables **last** and **nextToLast** in every iteration of the **for** loop so that every Fibonacci number is computed exactly once. In this case, every single value is computed only once no matter how big **n** is. Try to replace the recursive version with this version and see how fast you get the result when **n** is very big. By analyzing these examples, we should have no problem seeing that recursion usually has small code size, but sometimes the price it pays in the execution time is far too dear. In general, whenever both a recursive function and a non-recursive function are feasible, I usually go for the non-recursive version.

Now let's shift our attention to situations where recursion is absolutely necessary. One of the most well-known examples is the clone function for a binary search tree. Say at some point in the program you want to make two separate copies of the same tree, called **the Tree**, how do you do that? Many green programmers simply declare a new pointer to **tree** and make it point to **the Tree** just as follows:

```
BinarySearchTree *cloneTree = theTree;
```

Then they happily think that they have made an identical copy successfully and proceed to perform operations on **cloneTree**. The truth is that **cloneTree** simply points to what **the Tree** points to; changing either **cloneTree** or **the Tree** changes the only tree that exists. Therefore, to have two completely identical and independent trees, you need to use a function that recursively copies the right and left subtrees of the original tree to the new tree. The function may look something like this:

```
BinarySearchTree* BinarySearchTree::clone(BinaryNode *t){        //1
    if(t==NULL)                                                  //2
        return NULL;                                             //3
    else                                                        //4
        return BinaryNode(t->element, clone(t->left), clone(t->right));   //5
}
```

The first argument to **BinaryNode** is the data the node contains; the second argument is a pointer to **BinarySearchTree** which is the root of the left subtree; the third argument is a pointer to **BinarySearchTree** which is the root of the right subtree. Basically, this function returns a node which is identical to the root of the original tree by recursively constructing the left and the right subtrees until they hit the leaf nodes. As we can see, this operation is not achievable by using a non-recursive function because you do not know what the tree looks like in advance. In this type of situation, we can rely only on recursion. There are plenty of other examples to illustrate how powerful recursion is. As you become more experienced you will see how important and powerful it is.

4.4   Function Templates

Having discussed class templates, you should have some idea how function templates work. A function template accepts multiple data types. A classic example of a function template is to swap two arguments. Here it is:

```
template <class Any>  /* <typename Any> is a newer usage */
void swaps(Any &a, Any &b){
    Any temp;
    temp = a;
    a = b;
    b = temp;
}
```

You probably wonder if this function works with only rudimentary types such as **short**, **int**, and **char**. The way to test it is simple: you replace **Any** with a type and see if it works. For example, let's say **tt** is a struct and **t** and **t2** are its objects. Do you think we can do the following?

```
tt temp;
temp = t;
```

```
t = t2;
t2 = temp;
```

Of course we can. What about a class object? Suppose I have a class named **Score** and its two objects named **score** and **score2**. Do the following statements work?

```
Score temp;
temp = score;
score = score2;
score2 = temp;
```

The assignment operator between two objects of the same class performs a member-to-member copy, by default. So the statements above do work. You can have a pointer to **char** as one of the class data members and see if **swaps**() works. Pointers often give us surprises, so don't take everything for granted without experimentation.

4.5   Generality in Functions

As discussed in the previous section, a function template is able to replace multiple functions using genericity. This is one way to reduce code size. However, this type of situation does not come up often because you normally make a function deal with only certain argument types. Another way to replace many functions with one function is to *generalize* the meaning of the functions, and then write one or two functions that accommodate all of them. Sometimes this is achievable but not always. Usually to achieve this effect, a flag is necessary as one of the arguments of the function. As an example, let's consider the following scenario. You are writing a server that serves a client's requests. Assume there are exactly five request types a client may issue. You decide to write five functions to serve the requests. First you decide what the request is, then call the appropriate function. However, you can also write one function that servers a request given its identity, and you can merge the parts where the requests are doing the same things. So you simply have one function in which there are several **if** or **switch** blocks. This is actually in regards to the program I mentioned in the beginning of Section 4.2.

4.6 Function Pointer

I did not know that I could pass a function pointer as an argument of another function until my sophomore year in college. At first I was very excited because I thought that was something very useful, but to my disappointment, it never really proved useful and I hardly ever used it in any of the programs I wrote. Anyway, let's discuss this topic so that at least you know what it is. In essence, a function can use the function pointed to by the function pointer. A prototype of a function pointer looks like this:

```
/*
ptf is a pointer that points to a function that takes one char argument and
returns an int
*/
int (*ptf)(char);
```

Let me show you a sample program that illustrates the use of function pointers:

```
#include<iostream>
#include<cctype>   /* or <ctype.h> */
using namespace std;

int mike(char);
int vivien(char);
void analyze(int (*ptf)(char), char);

int main() {
    char grade;

    cout << "What is the grade you expect to get? ";
    cin >> grade;
    grade = tolower(grade);
    while(grade!='a' && grade!='b' && grade!='c' && grade!='d'
        && grade!='f') {
        cout << "Not a valid grade. Please enter again: ";
        cin >> grade;
        grade = tolower(grade);
    }
    cout << "Mike thinks that ";
    analyze(mike, grade);
```

```
        cout << " because Mike is dumb dumb...\n";
        cout << "Vivien thinks that ";
        analyze(vivien, grade);
        cout << " because Vivien is super smart!\n";
        return 0;
}

int mike(char grade) {
        int diff = 'f' - grade;
        return diff * 10;
}

int vivien(char grade) {
        int diff = 'f' - grade;
        return diff * 2;
}

void analyze(int (*ptf)(char), char grade) {
        cout << "it will take " << (*ptf)(grade);
        cout << " hours every week";
}
```

As you can see, **analyze**() simply takes the name of a function (with the same argument types and return type) as the first argument, and then uses its second argument to call that function. Inside **main**(), when you want to call **analyze**(), you pass the function address and the corresponding argument. The name of the function, as you may or may not yet realize, is actually the address of that function, allowing you to identify that function. You should be able to follow pretty much everything else in this program. A subtle point is that not only do you need to pass the function name, you also need to know its arguments to be able to use that function. You don't need to get the arguments to **ptf**() from the call to **analyze**() if you can get them somewhere else.

One scenario in which function pointers may come in handy is that at some point you do not know which function you need to call because it, for example, depends on the user input. The result of calling that function may need further processing. In this scenario, you may want to write a master function that takes another function as an argument. Depending on the user input, the call to the master function uses the appropriate function. Then the master function can get the results and process it accordingly. However, as you probably already see, you can simply use **if-else** statements to call the appropriate function, and then pass the results to another function to do more stuff.

4.7   Inline Function

Inline functions are a C++ feature designed to make programs run faster. Normal function calls have the program jump to another address and then return when the function finishes executing. Inline functions, however, make compiler replace their function calls with the actual function code. This way, the program does not have to jump to another location to execute code and then jump back, thereby increasing speed of running a program. The downside, obviously, is that the executable code is bigger because there are as many copies of function code as the number of function calls. Also, the speed gain usually is minimal, so you probably do not see any improvement anyway. In general, the best way to take advantage of inline functions is to make very short, frequently used functions inline. To use this feature, you need to prefix the keyword **inline** to the function definition. Here is a sample program illustrating the inline feature:

```
#include<iostream>
using namespace std;
#include<ctime>  /* or <time.h> */

inline double square(double x) { return x*x; }

int main(){
    double i,j,k,temp;
    int limit = 100;

    clock_t start = clock();
    for(i=0;i<limit;i+=0.5)
        for(j=0;j<limit;j+=0.5)
            for(k=0;k<limit;k+=0.5)
                temp=square(k);
    cout << (float)(clock() - start) / CLOCKS_PER_SEC << " seconds\n";
    return 0;
}
```

You can run this version several times, then take out the word "inline", then run the modified version several times. I ran this experiment and here is what I got:

With inline (in seconds)	Without inline (in seconds)
0.537	0.633
0.506	0.964
0.538	0.871

As you can see, proper use of inline functions does pay off in terms of program speed. Incidentally, C uses **#define** statement to provide the functionality of an inline function. For example, to get the product of two numbers, you do:

```
#define product(a,b) a*b
```

During compiling, the compiler substitutes a*b for every occurrence of product(a,b). If you do:

```
int i = product(3+4,4+5);
```

product(3+4,4+5) will be replaced with 3+4*4+5, yielding undesired results. Thus, it is generally advisable for you to use C++ inline functions or normal functions.

Also, any function defined in the class declaration becomes an inline function automatically. You still can make a function defined outside the class declaration an inline function by prefixing it with the keyword **inline**.

4.8 Operator Overloading

Operator overloading is perhaps one of the most powerful tools that C++ provides. The idea is making an operator work with multiple data types. For example, **cout** is a heavily overloaded function because you can use it to output an **int**, a **char**, and a **string**. However, when you want **cout** to work with user-defined class objects, you need to write a function to overload **cout** even further. Let's learn how to write an overloaded function.

Let's say you want to overload operators that define relations between two complex numbers, which include addition, subtraction, multiplication, and conjugation. For addition, you want to add two complex numbers and return the result to the invoking object. You can do the following:

```
Complex operator+(Complex & c);  /* inside class Complex */
Complex Complex::operator+(Complex & c) {      /* definition */
...
     return ...
}
```

Inside **main()**, let's say **a**, **b**, **c** are all instances of **Complex**. The following two lines mean the same thing:

```
a = b.operator+(c);
a = b + c;
```

The second assignment is a unique property of operators such as +, -, *, and /. It allows programmers to use operator notations so that they look friendlier. As you can see, you cannot make the functions **void** because you need to return the result for the assignment operator to work. An important point to note is that you can also do this:

```
a = a + b + c;
```

That's because the compiler sees the expression as **a = (a + b) + c** and evaluates **a + b** first. Then the result replaces **a + b**, turning the expression into **a = result + c**. This is analogous to **cout**'s ability to do **cout << ... << ...** On the other hand, let's say you want addition to work between a **Complex** object and an **int**, you can do the following:

```
Complex operator+(int n);  /* inside class Complex */
Complex Complex::operator+(int n) {  /* definition */
...
     return ...
}
```

But now you only can do

```
a = b + 5;
```

and not

```
a = 5 + b;
```

The compiler views expression **a** = **b** + 5 as equivalent to **a** = **b.operator+**(5), and won't recognize **a** = **5.operator+**(**b**). Next I will show you how you can make **a** = 5 + **b** work.

Let's discuss how *nonmember* functions interact with operators. In this case, you need two arguments because the function is independent of **Complex**. You can do the following:

```
Complex operator+(Complex & c, Complex & c2);    /* function prototype */
Complex operator+(Complex & c, Complex & c2) {   /* function definition */
...
      return ...
}
```

This is exactly how the aforementioned problem may be solved. If you want **a** = 5 + **b** to work, simply declare the first argument to be an **int** and the second argument to be a **Complex** object. On the other hand, let's say **a**, **b**, **c** are all objects of **Complex**. Then you only can do

```
a = b + c;
```

but not

```
a = b.operator+(c);
```

That's because **operator+**() is no longer a member of **Complex**. Another important point to note is that you may not be able to do:

```
a = a + b + c;
```

The assignment may or may not work depending on the implementations you are using. If the compiler complains, try taking out '&' in both function prototype and function definition or inserting a '&' between **Complex** and **operator+**. As you can see, member functions and nonmember functions have their advantages and disadvantages. From now on you should be able to make judicious decisions about overloading operators.

The following are some common operators that you may overload:

+	=	*=	>>=	>	&	>>	->	<=
-	==	/=	<<=	<	|	<<	->*	,
*	!=	%=	&=	!	^=	()	new	||
/	+=	>=	|=	&&	~=	[]	delete	^
%	-=	>>=	~					

new and **delete** are English words, but you still can do

```
... operatornew(...);
... operatordelete(...);
```

You can pretty much overload any operator the way we just discussed; however, for some of them you should not make their overloaded functions **void**, particularly <<. If you do so, the function no longer can use multiple operators in a single line, like cout << ... << ... Therefore, it is advisable for the overloaded function to return an object. Here are several general rules regarding operator overloading:

1. Nonmember functions must take exactly 2 arguments, and one of which must be a user-defined type (class or struct); member functions must have 0 or 1 argument (one operand is already a user-defined type).
2. You cannot alter operator context (e.g. cannot make a binary operator become a unary operator) or precedence.
3. You cannot create new operators.
4. You can use only member functions to overload operators =, ->, [], and ().

Here is a sample program that illustrates a member function overloading +:

```
#include <iostream>
using namespace std;

class Clock {
    int hours;
    int minutes;
public:
    Clock() {};
    Clock(int h, int m) { hours = h; minutes = m; }
```

```
        Clock operator+(Clock & t);
        int hr() { return hours; }
        int min() { return minutes; }
};

Clock Clock::operator+(Clock & t) {
        Clock sum;
        sum.hours = hours + t.hours + (minutes + t.minutes)/60;
        sum.minutes = (minutes + t.minutes) % 60;
        return sum;
}

ostream & operator<<(ostream & os, Clock & t){
        os << t.hr() << " hours, " << t.min() << " minutes";
        return os;
}

int main() {
        Clock a(1, 40);
        Clock b(3, 29);
        Clock c(2, 19);
        cout << a << endl << b << endl << c << endl;
        a = a + b + c;
        cout << a << endl;
        return 0;
}
```

Here is a sample program that illustrates a nonmember function overloading +:

```
#include <iostream>
using namespace std;

class Clock {
        int hours;
        int minutes;
public:
        Clock() {};
        Clock(int h, int m) { hours = h; minutes = m; }
        int hr() { return hours; }
        int min() { return minutes; }
```

```
        int set_hr(int h) { hours = h; }
        int set_min(int m) { minutes = m; }
};

Clock & operator+(Clock & t, Clock & t2) {
        Clock sum;
        sum.set_hr(t.hr() + t2.hr() + (t.min()+t2.min())/60);
        sum.set_min((t.min()+t2.min()) % 60);
        return sum;
}

ostream & operator<<(ostream & os, Clock & t){
        os << t.hr() << " hours, " << t.min() << " minutes";
        return os;
}

int main() {
        Clock a(1, 40);
        Clock b(3, 29);
        Clock c(2, 19);
        cout << a << endl << b << endl << c << endl;
        a = a + b + c;
        cout << a << endl;
        return 0;
}
```

Try overloading operators such as -, *, and >> as an exercise, will ya?

4.9   Traps and Tips

- You may declare a function prototype, member or nonmember, without ever defining it. There will no problem if you don't use that function. If you do use it, however, then you need to define it.
- Use **inline** instead of #**define** to define short functions.
- Use **const** instead of #**define** to define constants.
- *Whenever calling a function, think about whether you want the arguments passed by reference or by value.*

- *Function preconditions and postconditions should always be preserved.* When you complete a function, think about whether it can deal with every possible value in its arguments without crashing. Think about what it should do when it receives incorrect arguments.

Out of our five fingers, the fingernail of our middle finger grows the most quickly.

CHAPTER 5

Debugging

Frenchmen De Wilson and Bugging Jay built the first chrono-sphere in the world. When everything was ready and the lab filled with journalists and broadcasters, they pushed the red button excitedly, but nothing happened.
"What the…what's wrong?"
"Let's check the chrono belt and the quantum transmission system again."
Somewhere inside the system got stuck a big cockroach. They took it out and everything worked.
The spectators exclaimed, "Wow, what do you say we name the act of fixing machines 'DeBugging' to honor you guys?"

So whenever you are trying to fix your program, you are essentially doing what De and Bugging did. In fact, the English prefix "de" came to mean "removal" to honor their extraordinary feat back in 2059.

Yeah right.

5.1   Syntax Error Versus Logic Error

Every programmer knows that debugging is a time-consuming nightmare, so it makes a good candidate for programmers to learn how to deal with. There are generally two types of errors: syntax errors and logic errors. Syntax errors occur when a program's syntax does not conform to the grammar of a programming language, and the compiler cannot compile the source file. Logic errors occur when a program does not do what the programmer expects it to do. Syntax errors are usually easy to fix; the real pains in the neck are logic errors. Freeing a program of logic errors is almost always what a programmer ends up doing, eventually successfully or failingly. Next we will explore different ways to debug.

5.2 Debugging Using Print Statements

Using the output ability of a program is generally useful for debugging. It is very useful in three situations while a program is running. In the first situation, the program hangs and must be terminated forcibly. To find out the cause, we can insert print statements in different places and run the program again. Doing so generally enables us to locate where the hanging occurs. In the second situation, the program exits after generating a segmentation fault. Most programmers would probably agree that a segmentation fault is the most annoying and elusive bug. Again, inserting print statements in several places generally helps you see where this fault is generated. A detailed discussion about segmentation fault will be given in Chapter 9. In the third case, the program runs infinitely and does not exit until the operating system runs out of memory. Two of the most common sources of this problem are an infinite loop and infinite recursion.

In any case, you need to make sure you "flush" the outputs in your print statements to make them meaningful. See Section 16.2 for more details.

5.3 Debugging Using Debugging Tools

There is a wealth of debugging tools in the Internet and the book market, some free of charge and some rather costly. They include GDB (The GNU Project Debugger), DDD (Data Display Debugger), SAS/C Debugger, Microsoft Visual C++ Debugger, etc. Debugging tools are usually very useful in tracking down a bug, so I recommend that you use it. The debugger I have been using is called GDB and I strongly recommend using it. It has only a few easy-to-remember commands. Using it correctly, you are almost guaranteed to locate bugs in a short period of time. If you use a UNIX machine that has GDB installed, you can do "man gdb" to learn about it. If not, you can find out how to use it on the Internet or in a bookstore. I recommend that you try out some of the common debuggers and stick to one of them for the rest of your programming career.

5.4 Common Causes of Bugs

Here is a list of common causes of bugs and suggested ways to prevent them:

- **Incorrect use of variables**, including using C++ keywords as variable names and confusing classes' names with their instances', is a common source of bugs. Stick to a naming convention and do not use C++

keywords to name anything (refer to <u>Appendix A</u> for a list of C++'s keywords). If you use a C++ keyword to name a variable, the errors the compiler gives may not indicate the cause directly and it may take some time before you realize it.

- **Preconditions of a function** are not preserved right before calling it. For example, if a function does not handle certain arguments which are passed to it, errors result. So make sure the function can deal with them. I can't emphasize enough how important it is. When you write a function, put its preconditions and postconditions inside comments and make sure it can deal with all types of arguments passed to it.

- **Disorganized style of programming** often results in incorrect nested loops or omissions of necessary brackets. So make sure you adopt good style, especially indent lines appropriately.

- **Unexpected program flow control** is a common cause of logic bugs. For example, if you use **if-else** statements, think about what they should be followed by. Given different conditions, the program flow at runtime can be totally different. During the design phase, go through each possible program flow to see if it's correct.

- **Incomplete understanding of the programming language** is a serious problem. If you use a statement or a standard function, make sure you know exactly what it does. For instance, **cin >>** skips spaces, tabs, and newlines but **cin.get(char)** doesn't. Many C++ standard functions are very useful, but when you are about to use them, know exactly what they do, what their preconditions are, and how they deal with exceptions. *You need to know your tools before you use them.*

- In a big program, **incomplete knowledge of the state of variables** at any point in time could cause major problems. As an example, sometimes we use an array to store data, then at one point we want to do some operation on it in order to get information we need, then we forget to restore the array to its previous state. Sometimes we shouldn't restore it but we accidentally do. In either case, bugs result. To keep disasters from happening, you need to be clear on the state of variables at any time when the program is running.

On average, human hair grows about 6 inches a year.

CHAPTER 6

Arrays Versus Pointers

"I thought I gave you detailed pointers on how your sales pitch should go," yelled the sales manager.
"Well your pointers to the array of high-sounding words simply didn't cut it," answered Grace calmly.

Fortunately, a pointer in C++ points to only one address, not an array of addresses.

6.1   Differences between Arrays and Pointers

An array is an allocation of resources during compile time. Upon knowing the size and type of the array, the compiler allocates corresponding resources of that specific size for that specific type. You can no longer change its size during run time. A pointer, however, exhibits different attributes. C users can specify the size via **malloc()**, and C++ users can do so by using the keyword **new**. A pointer is useful when the programmer does not know in advance the size of the type needed. For example, if you want to write a program that creates however many objects of points specified by user's command line, you can declare a pointer pointing to **point**, then use **malloc()** or **new** to allocate that many objects once the user enters that number.

Another way a pointer is useful is when you need compiler to see an object which is not initialized by the constructor of that class. For example, you can create a pointer pointing to an object of a class without using its constructor. If you simply create an object of a class, you need to specify its arguments according to its constructor. In a situation where you don't know the arguments of the constructor yet, using a pointer is a good option.

In the first year of programming, I usually used arrays. After I learned C's **malloc()** and C++'s **new**, I began to rely on dynamic allocation of resources. Since dynamic memory allocation is important, below we will see how to use **malloc()** and **new**.

43

6.2 Higher Order of Array via malloc()

malloc() is a popular library function in C. A programmer knowing how to use **malloc**() has no problem creating a one-dimensional array. However, what about two-dimensional or even three-dimensional array? The point of using **malloc**() is to dynamically allocate space because in some situations the programmer has no way of knowing how many variables he needs until later. Here is an example of how to use **malloc**() to create a two-dimensional array:

```
char **peers;
peers=(char**)malloc(3*sizeof(char*)); /* peers contains 3 char* */
peers[0]="the first one"; /* initialize the first char* */
peers[1]="the second one";    /* initialize the second char* */
peers[2]="the third one"; /* initialize the third char* */
```

As we can see, **peers** is a two-dimensional array, but how are the data stored? For example, what will **peers[0][5]** give you? It will give you the letter "i" because it is the sixth letter in **peers[0]**.

For those who are still confused by the way higher order **malloc**() works, here is an example of how to use **malloc**() to create a three-dimensional array:

```
char ***peers;
peers=(char***)malloc(3*sizeof(char**));  /* peers contains 3 char** */
peers[0]=(char**)malloc(3*sizeof(char*)); /* peers[0] contains 3 char* */
peers[1]=(char**)malloc(4*sizeof(char*)); /* peers[1] contains 4 char* */
peers[2]=(char**)malloc(5*sizeof(char*)); /* peers[2] contains 5 char* */

/* initialize all char* variables, 12 total */
peers[0][0]="guys";
peers[0][1]="it";
peers[0][2]="all";
peers[1][0]="comes";
peers[1][1]="down";
peers[1][2]="to";
peers[1][3]="dealing";
peers[2][0]="with";
peers[2][1]="people";
peers[2][2]="david";
peers[2][3]="and";
```

peers[2][4]="jim";

If you want to deallocate memory allocated by using **malloc()**, use **free()**, not **delete**.

6.3 Higher Order of Array via **new**

C++ provides **new** operator which is a better way to dynamically allocate memory than **malloc()**. You can use either one but **new** is recommended, in part due to its conciseness. Here is a demonstration of how to declare a two-dimensional array dynamically using **new**:

```
int **a2Darray;
a2Darray = new int*[3];
a2Darray[0] = new int[1];
a2Darray[1] = new int[2];
a2Darray[2] = new int[3];
a2Darray[0][0] = 1;
a2Darray[1][0] = 2;
a2Darray[1][1] = 3;
a2Darray[2][0] = 4;
a2Darray[2][1] = 5;
a2Darray[2][2] = 6;
```

As we can see, **a2Darray** is a two-dimensional array with a total of 6 elements. Each element can be accessed via [][] notation. By the same token, a three-dimensional array looks like:

```
int ***a;
a = new int**[3];
a[0] = new int*[1];
a[1] =new int*[2];
a[2] = new int*[3];
a[0][0] = new int[2];
a[1][0] = new int[2];
a[1][1] = new int[2];
a[2][0] = new int[3];
a[2][1] = new int[3];
a[2][2] = new int[3];
```

```
a[0][0][0] = 0;
a[0][0][1] = 1;
a[1][0][0] = 2;
a[1][0][1] = 3;
...
```

To deallocate memory allocated by using **new**, use **delete**. Using **delete** on a pointer that did not use **new** is not allowed.

6.4   Why Start at Index 0 While You Can Start at 1?

Although an array starts at index 0, sometimes starting at 1 is a lot easier for programmers to visualize the running of the program in mind. For example, I wrote a program that creates a maze and each spot in the maze has its own attributes such as whether its right wall is down and what its neighbors are. It is highly desirable that the first spot in the maze has index 1 and identifier 1 and the second spot has index 2 and identifier 2, and so on. Doing so eliminates confusion which often results in bugs. Whenever I want to traverse all the spots in the maze, the index in the **for** loop starts at 1. Whenever I want to access a spot with a particular identifier, I can be rest assured that the spot can be accessed via the same index as the identifier.

An oyster makes pearls when an irritant gets stuck between its mantle and shell, so at a pearl's center lies the foreign substance.

CHAPTER 7

The Standard Template Library

A student walked into the professor's office.
"Professor Frankenstein, in class *today you told us we can store all our data in an array, then sort them, but we don't know the size of the array in advance."*
"Good day, Vika. Let's see here.. You can use dynamic allocation to deal with size problem and you can use bubble sort, selection sort, quick sort, or any other type of sort you are comfortable with."
"I know, but why not just use a vector to store data dynamically and use its sort function someone else has already written for us?"
"Uh…I never knew there is such thing as a vector."
"It does exist. It is one of the containers defined in the STL."
"STL? Containers?? What the $#@%??? Nobody ever told me that…"*

So you see, STL is a cool tool you should be equipped with, in case you don't have it yet.

The Standard Template Library, or STL, provides useful class templates called *containers*. A container can contain many objects of the same type, and different containers have different mechanisms to store and retrieve data. The goal of using a container is to store multiple objects in one object and to manipulate them efficiently. The word "template" refers to STL's ability to handle objects of many types, just like a class template does. At times your program may need to store many data objects dynamically, and using a container may be a good idea. This chapter will cover some of the most common container types, including **vector**, **list**, **queue**, **stack**, and **set**. In my opinion, **vector** is the most useful container because it allows the size of its objects to vary dynamically, growing as elements are added and shrinking as elements are removed. It also supports random access to elements, unlike **stack** or **queue**. Finally, it is very easy to use. Therefore, make sure you know at least **vector**.

7.1 Basic Container Properties

The following table describes basic properties of containers such as constructors and functions, common to all container types. In the table, C represents a container type, including its identifier, such as **vector<string>** and **list<int>**; **a** and **b** represent objects of C.

Expression	Explanation
C::iterator a	a is an iterator of C
C a;	creates a container object named a
C a(b);	a uses copy constructor to initialize its contents to b's contents
C a = b;	a's contents are initialized to b's contents
a.size()	returns the number of elements
a.begin()	returns an iterator pointing to the first element
a.end()	returns an iterator pointing to the place immediately past the last element
a == b	returns true if a and b have the same size and each element in a is the same as the corresponding element in b; returns false otherwise
a != b	returns false if a and b have the same size and each element in a is the same as the corresponding element in b; returns true otherwise
a.swap(b)	swaps the contents of a and those of b

7.2 Basic Sequence Properties

Out of the eleven container types, **vector, stack, queue, deque, list**, and **priority_queue** are also known as sequences. A sequence, as its name suggests, has the property that its elements are arranged in linear order, which means operations such as removing and inserting elements at particular locations become feasible. In the following table, C represents a container type, including its identifier, such as **vector<string>** and **list<int>**; **a** represents an object of C; **n** is an integer; **c** is a value of the identifier; **i** and **j** are iterators. Here is something you must note: **a** is an object of C and **c** is a value of C's identifier. For example, in the statement

vector<string> concert;

concert is **a** and "Symphony" is an example of **c**.

Expression	Explanation
C a(i, j);	creates a sequence initialized to the contents of range [i, j)
C a(n, c);	creates a sequence of n copies of c
a.erase(i, j);	erases the contents of range [i, j)
a.erase(p);	erases the element p points to
a.clear();	erases all elements
a.insert(p, c);	inserts before p one copy of c
a.insert(p, n, c);	inserts before p n copies of c
a.insert(p, i, j);	inserts before p elements of range [i, j)

7.3 Vector and List

Because **vector** and **list** have many functions in common, I will cover them both in this section. You need to include <vector> in the header to use **vector**, and <list> in the header to use **list**. Followed are three tables showing how to use **vector** and **list**. **C** represents a container type, including its identifier, such as vector<string> and list<int>; **a** represents an object of type C; **n** is an integer; **c** is a value of the identifier; **p** is an iterator.

The following table shows expressions applied to both **vector** and **list**:

Expression	Explanation
a.front()	returns the first element
a.back()	returns the last element
a.push_back(c)	adds c to the end
a.pop_back()	removes the element from the end

The following table shows expressions applied to **vector** but not **list**:

Expression	Explanation
a[n]	returns nth element
a.at(n)	returns nth element

The following table shows **list**'s functions:

Function	Explanation
void merge(list<C> & a)	merges list a with the invoking list to form a sorted list, stored in the invoking list. Both lists must be sorted, or the resulting list is not necessarily sorted. a is left empty.
void splice(iterator p, list<C> & a)	inserts before p the contents of a, and a is left empty
void sort()	sorts the list using operator <
void unique()	if consecutive identical elements exist, they are reduced to a single element
void remove(const C & c)	removes all occurrences of c from the invoking list
void reverse()	reverses the order of the elements in the invoking list

Let's see how vector works by looking at the following program.

```
#include <iostream>
using namespace std;
#include <vector>
#include <string>

struct record {
    string name;
    string author;
};
vector<record> vr;
void showMenu();
void add();
void remove();
void empty();
void show();

int main(){
    char input;
    cout << "********** Welcome to database **********\n";
    while(true) {
        showMenu();
```

```
        cin >> input;
        cin.get();
        switch(input){
            case 'a': add();
                break;
            case 'b': remove();
                break;
            case 'c': empty();
                break;
            case 'd': show();
                break;
            case 'e': cout << "Bye.\n";
                 return 0;
                break;
            default:  cout << endl;
        }
        cout<<endl;
    }
    return 0;
}

void showMenu() {
    cout << "a. Add a book.\n";
    cout << "b. Remove a book.\n";
    cout << "c. Empty database.\n";
    cout << "d. Show the number of books currently in database.\n";
    cout << "e. Quit.\n\n";
    cout << "Please enter a choice: ";
}

void add() {
    record temp;
    string name, author;
    cout << "Please enter the name of the book: ";
    getline(cin, name);
    cout << "Please enter the name of the author: ";
    getline(cin, author);
    temp.name = name;
    temp.author = author;
    vr.push_back(temp);
```

```
        cout << "The book has been added.\n";
}

void remove() {
    string name;
    vector<record>::iterator vri;
    cout << "Please enter the name of the book: ";
    getline(cin, name);
    for(vri = vr.begin(); vri != vr.end(); vri++) {
        if((*vri).name == name) {
            vr.erase(vri);
            cout << "The book has been removed.\n";
            return;
        }
    }
    cout << "The book is not found.\n";
}

void empty() {
    vr.clear();
    cout << "All records are cleared.\n";
}

void show() {
    cout << "The number of books in current database is " << vr.size() <<
".\n";
}
```

This example covers only several common functions. Given the prototypes and descriptions of the functions, you should be able to experiment with the rest on your own. **Vector** is especially useful when you want to store many objects somewhere but you do not know how many in advance.

There are two functions I want you to know about because at times they can be very useful: **random_shuffle**() and **sort**(). They both require that the container support random access, such as a **vector**. The **random_shuffle**() takes two iterators specifying a range and rearranges the contents within that range arbitrarily. So if **hollywood** is an instance of **vector<Star>**, you can do

```
random_shuffle(hollywood.begin(), hollywood.end());
```

to mess up the order of elements in **hollywood**. There are two versions of **sort()**. The first one takes two iterators that specify a range and sorts the contents within that range based on the operator <. If the container elements are user-defined types, then you need to define **operator<()** that returns a bool. The following is an example of **operator<()** definition:

```
bool operator<(Star star, Star star2) {
    if(star.wealth < star2.wealth)
        return true;
    else if(star.wealth == star2.wealth && star.height < star2.height)
        return true;
    return false;
}
```

This function returns true if the first **star** is less wealthy than the second one, or if they are equally wealthy the first **star** is shorter; it returns false otherwise. Here is the function call to use **sort()**:

```
sort(hollywood.begin(), hollywood.end());
```

After sorting is done, the first element in **hollywood** will be the least wealthy.

The second version of **sort()** takes two iterators that indicate a range and a third argument which is a function address so that sorting is done based on that function instead of operator <. The following is such a function:

```
bool newSort(Star star, Star star2) {
    if(star.wealth < star2.wealth)
        return true;
    return false;
}
```

If you use **newSort()** to sort, then the first element of the resulting vector will be the least wealthy. But if there are more than one such star, there is no knowing how they are ordered. Here is a function call to use **newSort()** to sort:

```
sort(hollywood.begin(), hollywood.end(), newSort);
```

Now let's see a program illustrating how to use **list**:

```
#include <iostream>
using namespace std;
#include <list>

template <typename T>
ostream & operator<<(ostream & os, list<T> a){
    list<T>::iterator lii;
    for(lii = a.begin(); lii != a.end(); lii++)
        os << *lii << ' ';
    return os;
}

int main() {
    list<int> l1;
    list<int> l2(6,3);
    list<int> l3(l2);

    int temp[] = {8,4,1,3};
    l1.insert(l1.end(), temp, temp+4);
    l3.insert(l3.begin(), temp, temp+3);
    cout << "List #1: " << l1 << endl;
    cout << "List #2: " << l2 << endl;
    cout << "List #3: " << l3 << endl;
    l3.splice(l3.begin(), l1);
    cout << "List #3 after splice: " << l3 << endl;
    l3.remove(1);
    cout << "List #3 w/t 1: " << l3 << endl;
    l3.sort();
    cout << "List #3 after sort: " << l3 << endl;
    l3.unique();
    cout << "List #3 after unique: " << l3 << endl;
    l1.insert(l1.end(), temp, temp+4);
    l1.sort();
    l3.merge(l1);
    cout << "List #3 after merge: " << l3 << endl;
    l3.unique();
    cout << "List #3 after unique: " << l3 << endl;
```

```
    return 0;
}
```

Run the program and you should pretty much understand each line of output. **List** provides functions such as **merge()** and **sort()** which can prove helpful at times. One example is that a group of 10 people want to buy lottery, which consists of 6 numbers. You can receive 6 numbers from each of them and then use **sort()**, **merge()**, and **unique()** to get a clean sequence of unique numbers, which come from all 10 people's opinions. Another example is that you have two or more dictionaries and you want to combine them all into one single dictionary by removing identical entries via **sort()**, **merge()**, and **unique()**.

7.4   Queue and Stack

Most of you know should already how a **stack** and a **queue** work. Now that STL already provides template classes for **stack** and **queue**, you can go ahead and take advantage of them whenever you need them. Since the **queue** and **stack** have much in common conceptually, I will cover them both in this section. You need to include <stack> (formerly <stack.h>) in the header to use **stack** and <queue> (formerly <queue.h>) to use the **queue**. They are both more restrictive than **vector** because you cannot iterate through their elements and you cannot randomly access any element. You can only use basic operations that are defined for them. In the following two tables, **C** represents a container type including its identifier (i.e. **vector<string>**); **c** is a value of the identifier. The following table shows the functions of the **queue** template class:

Function	Explanation
C & front()	returns the element at the front of the queue
C & back()	returns the element at the back of the queue
void push(const C & c)	inserts c to the back of the queue
void pop()	removes the element at the front of the queue
int size() const;	returns the number of elements in the queue
bool empty() const;	returns true if the queue is empty; returns false otherwise

The following table shows the functions of the **stack** template class:

Function	Explanation
C & top()	returns the element at the top of the stack
void push(const C & c)	inserts c to the top of the stack
void pop()	removes the element at the top of the stack
int size() const;	returns the number of elements in the stack
bool empty() const;	returns true if the stack is empty; returns false otherwise

It is very straightforward to use functions provided by <queue> and <stack>, and you should already be familiar with them if you have taken a data structure course.

7.5   Set

Set is one of the associative containers. An associative container associates a data item with a key and uses the key to find the corresponding data item. There are several properties that mathematics defines for a set. The union of two sets is a set that combines everything two sets cover, and each element is unique. The intersection of two sets is a set that consists of only the values that are common to both sets. The difference of two sets is a set that consists of the values that the first set has but the second one doesn't. To use **set**, include <set> (formerly <set.h>) in the header. In the table, **abegin** is an iterator pointing to the starting position of **set A**; **aend** is an iterator pointing to the ending position of **set A**; **bbegin** is an iterator pointing to the starting position of **set B**; **bend** is an iterator pointing to the ending position of **set B**; **oiterator** is an output iterator identifying the location for the resulting set to copy to. **i** and **j** are iterators.

Function	Description
set_union(abegin, aend, bbegin, bend, oiterator);	returns the union of range [abegin, aend) and range [bbegin, bend)
set_intersection(abegin, aend, bbegin, bend, oiterator);	returns the intersection of range [abegin, aend) and range [bbegin, bend)
set_difference(abegin, aend, bbegin, bend, oiterator);	returns the difference of range [abegin, aend) and range [bbegin, bend)
A.lower_bound(k);	returns an iterator to the first element whose key is equal to or greater than k
A.upper_bound(k);	returns an iterator to the first element whose key is greater than k
A.insert(v);	inserts v in A
A.insert(i, j);	inserts range [i, j] in A

One thing you may be wondering about is how the fifth argument of the first three functions works. It is an output iterator, which specifies the location to store the resulting set. If it is **ostream_iterator**, that means that the set is printed onscreen. However, if you want to copy the resulting set to a new set, say **C**, then you can use **insert_iterator**. Here is a sample program illustrating how **set** works:

```cpp
#include <iostream>
#include <string>
#include <set>
using namespace std;

ostream & operator<<(ostream & os, set<string> s) {
    set<string>::iterator sti;
    for(sti = s.begin(); sti != s.end(); sti++)
        os << *sti << ' ';
    return os;
}

int main() {
    set<string> set1, set2, set3;
    int i;

    string ts="value#";
    string res;
    for(i=0;i<5;i++){
        res=ts;
        res+=('a'+i);
        set1.insert(res);
    }
    for(i=0;i<10;i++){
        res=ts;
        res+=('a'+i);
        set2.insert(res);
    }

    cout<<"set1: "<<set1<<"\nlower_bound: "<<*(set1.lower_bound("value#b"))<<
                "\nupper_bound: "<<*(set1.upper_bound("value#b"))<<endl;
    cout<<"set2: "<<set2<<endl;
    set_union(set1.begin(), set1.end(), set2.begin(), set2.end(),
```

```
            insert_iterator<set<string> >(set3, set3.begin()));
    cout<<"set3: "<<set3<<endl;
    return 0;
}
```

As you can see from the program output, **set3** covers everything **set1** and **set2** cover. Now that you have acquired one more powerful tool, STL, you should not be afraid to use it from now on. Use it well and it can solve many problems for you.

A CD contains error-checking code that can handle many scratches on its surface. So don't worry when you scratch it.

CHAPTER 8

String

Once upon a time, Tailand and Chiland were ready to launch a full-scale projectile war against each other. Each of them was using only one bomb launcher in the war, but their implementations were different. Tailand was using a character array to manage the launcher, while Chiland, being more clever, was using a string to manage their bomber. The war thus began. In the beginning the war was a tossup, but at one moment Chiland decided to do something different.

"Insert two more A-bombs right after the bomb indexed at the 6th place in the launcher. Replace the second to the last bomb with an H-Bomb. Switch the order of all fission bombs with that of fusion bombs."
"Well do"
Tailand became agitated.
"What are we going to do? We cannot insert or append any of our bombs in the launcher once we initialize them. What in God's name are we going to do?"

Bombing from Chiland kept on going. They were able to dynamically change the types of bombs to their hearts' content. Eventually Tailand sank deep in the ocean and never surfaced again.

Now you should know clearly why you should use a string instead of a character array.

8.1   Character Array in C

First of all, the concept of a string in C is always a character array. Standard C++ library, however, includes the **string** class that provides common manipulations of a character array. This chapter will introduce you to many common functions that you can use to manipulate a string, which is guaranteed to prove useful in your programming career.

8.2 C++ String Class

A C++ string class object is very easy to manipulate. For example, you can append it with another string, a character, or a pointer to characters with very little hassle. You can insert another string into a string. You can erase a substring from a string. Being aware of the methods string provides is very important because string is one of the most versatile types to store data. Many programmers tend to use a structure or a class to store data, but is a structure or a class the only way to store data? What about using a string with delimiters separating the data items? For example, let's say that a bank customer has the following information: id, account creation date, account type, email, password, and balance, where each data item is either a number or a string. We can use a structure or a class to encapsulate all the data items. On the other hand, we can also use a string, with a character being the delimiter, to represent a client. An example is (# is the delimiter): "3456#3/17/1979#prima#jo@yahoo.com#password#99999.99#".

Then we can simply create functions to handle parsing of this string and retrieving a particular data item of this customer. It may or may not be a good idea, but at least it's a possibility and may come in handy in some situation. Another example is using a string to store a path in say, a network, represented by edges and nodes. The string contains a series of integers, representing the nodes of the network, separated by a delimiter. Some programmers might use an array of integers to store a path, but a string comes in handy here. A path with nodes 6 3 8 1 3 39 2 8 could be "6#3#8#1#3#39#2#8#" instead of eight integers in an array. Using a string is much easier because a path could be shorter or longer; using an **int** array, however, needs to dynamically allocate resources. Adding integers and delimiters in a string are easy operations, at least to programmers (underlying structure uses dynamic allocation as well). Also, strings could minimize confusion and code size of a program.

8.2.1 Constructors

Since **string** is such a useful class, it helps to learn the functions it provides. First, let's learn its constructors. There are six constructors **string** provides. The following table shows the constructor prototypes and the corresponding descriptions. The string class uses **string::npos** as a symbolic constant for the maximum possible length of a string.

Constructor	Description
string()	creates an empty string object
string(const string s, int n, int n2)	creates a string and initializes it to contents starting at index n spanning n2 characters in s
string(const char *cs)	creates a string and initializes it to cs
string(int n, char c)	creates a string and initializes it to n's c
string(const char *cs, int n)	creates a string and initializes it to the first n elements in cs; if n is too big the string will contain garbage data
string(pt b, pt e)	initializes string object to the values of range [b, e); b and e can be pointers pointing to some element in a char array

Let's pay attention to the second constructor as it is useful. Here is its real proto-type:

string(const string & s, int pos = 0; int n = string::npos);

The second argument, **pos**, specifies the starting copying position. The third argument, **n**, specifies how many characters should be copied to the invoking object. If you just give the first argument, the entire s is copied to the invoking object. If the third argument exceeds the length of the available characters, the constructor simply copies the remaining string starting at **pos**; it doesn't give you garbage data. Here are several examples:

```
string Cindy("Cindy has inner beauty");
string ex(Cindy); /* ex is "Cindy has inner beauty" */
string ex2(Cindy, 6);  /* ex2 is "has inner beauty" */
string ex3(Cindy, 6, 3);  /* ex3 is "has" */
string ex4(Cindy, 6, 1000);  /* ex4 is "has inner beauty" */
```

8.2.2 Test for Equality

To test equality of two string objects, use == or != operators. If two strings, A and B, are exactly the same, then (A == B) returns true and (A != B) returns false. Note that these operators can also be used on **char** arrays. So you can compare two strings, one string and one **char** array, and two **char** arrays. For C users, you can use **strcmp(char*, char*)**.

8.2.3 Append Operators

There are many situations where you want to append a string to another string. You can use += operator, which lets you append a string, a **char** array, or a character to another string, as the following prototypes show:

```
string & operator+=(const string & s);
string & operator+=(const char *cs);
string & operator+=(char c);
```

Here are several examples:

```
string a = "intentions ";
string b = "speak louder than ";
char *c = "actions";
char d = 'd';
a = a + b;  /* a is "intentions speak louder than " */
a = a + c;  /* a is "intentions speak louder than actions" */
a = "intentions ";
a = a + d;  /* a is "intentions d" */
```

8.2.4 The append() Functions

Closely related to += operator are the **append()** functions which allow you to append a string, a character array, or a character to a string. They work like += operator but they are more powerful in that they allow you to, for example, append multiple identical characters.

```
string & append(const string & s);
string & append(const string & s, int pos, int n);
string & append(int n, char c);
string & append(const char *cs);
string & append(const char *cs, int n);
```

The first function simply appends **s** to the invoking object. The second one appends **s**, starting at index **pos** and spanning **n** characters in **s**. It will not go beyond the end of **s** if **n** is too big. The third one appends **n**'s **c**. The fourth one appends **cs**. The fifth one appends the first **n** characters in **cs**.

Here are several examples:

```
string a = "Robert ";
string b = "is not ";
char *c = "superb ";
char d = 'd';
a.append(b);  /* a is "Robert is not " */
a = "Robert ";
a.append(b, 0, 3);  /* a is "Robert is " */
a.append(c, 6);  /* a is "Robert is superb" */
a = "Robert ";
a.append(5, d);  /* a is "Robert ddddd" */
```

8.2.5   The substr() Function

You can use this function to return a substring of the invoking object. Here's its prototype:

```
string substr(int pos = 0, int n = string::npos) const;
```

It returns a string copied starting at index **pos** for **n** characters or up to the end of the invoking string object, whichever comes first. If only **pos** is supplied, the function returns the string copied starting at index **pos** until the end of the invoking string object. If no arguments are supplied, the function simply returns a string identical to the invoking string object. Here are a couple of examples:

```
string s = "thanks for help, ying";
cout << s.substr(7, 3) << endl;  /* print "for" */
cout << s.substr(17) << endl;  /* print "ying" */
```

8.2.6   The insert() Functions

The **insert()** functions allow you to insert a character, a character array, a string, or multiple characters into a string, given the starting position. Here are the prototypes of the most commonly used **insert()** functions:

```
string & insert(int pos, const string & s);
string & insert(int pos, const char *cs);
string & insert(int pos, const char *cs, int n);
string & insert(int pos, int n, char c);
```

The first function inserts **s** in the invoking object at index **pos**. The second one inserts **cs** in the invoking object at index **pos**. The third one inserts the first **n** characters in **cs** in the invoking object at index **pos**. The fourth one inserts **n**'s **c** in the invoking object at index **pos**. Here are several examples:

```
string a = "Petrina ";
string b = "dogs";
char *c = "loves cats";
char d = '.';
a.insert(8, b); /* a is "Petrina dogs" */
a.insert(8, c, 6); /* a is "Petrina loves dogs" */
a.insert(7, 3, d); /* a is "Petrina... loves dogs" */
```

8.2.7 The assign() Functions

There exist **assign()** functions that allow you to assign a string, a substring, or a succession of identical characters to a string. However, you can use assignment operators and **append()** functions for the same purpose. I personally never used **assign()**.

8.2.8 The replace() Functions

You can replace a substring of a string with a given string or **char** array by using the **replace()** functions. There is a variety of the **replace()** functions and I will just show you the most useful ones. Here are their prototypes:

```
string & replace(int pos, int n, const string & s);
string & replace(int pos, int n, const char* cs);
string & replace(int pos, int n, const char* cs, int n2, int n3);
string & replace(int pos, int n, int n2, char c);
```

The first function replaces with **s** contents from index **pos** spanning **n** characters. The second one replaces with **cs** contents from index **pos** spanning **n** characters. The third one replaces contents from index **pos** spanning **n** characters with the first **n3** characters of **cs** starting at n2. The fourth one replaces contents from index **pos** spanning **n** characters with **n2** **c**'s. Here are several examples:

```
string a = "Best Worst";
string b = "wishes to Demon";
```

```
char *c = "Lali";
char *c2 = "Dell";
char d = '~';
a.replace(5, 5, b);  /* a is "Best wishes to Demon" */
a.replace(15, 5, c);  /* a is "Best wishes to Lali" */
a.replace(15, 1, c2, 0, 1);  /* a is "Best wishes to Dali" */
a.replace(19, 0, 3, d);  /* a is "Best wishes to Dali~~~" */
```

8.2.9   The find() Functions

You can use the **find()** functions to locate the first occurrence of a string, a character array, or a character. If the target is not found, the functions return **string::npos**. These functions are useful in a situation where you need to parse a string which contains some sort of delimiter.

```
int find(const string & s, int pos = 0) const;
int find(const char *cs, int pos = 0) const;
int find(char c, int pos = 0) const;
```

The first function searches the invoking object for **s** starting at index **pos** and returns the index where **s** is first located. The second one searches invoking object for **cs** starting at index **pos** and returns the index where **cs** is first located. The third one searches invoking object for **c** starting at index **pos** and returns the index where **c** is first located. As noted before, if the target is not found, all functions return **string::npos**. Here are several examples:

```
string s = "Ja yo Afu! Yo yo yo!";
string s2 = "yo";
char *s3 = "you";
char c = '!';
unsigned int temp;  /* string::npos is a big number */
temp = s.find(s2);  /* temp is 3 */
temp = s.find(s2, 4);  /* temp is 14 */
temp = s.find(s3);  /* temp is string::npos */
temp = s.find(s3, 6);  /* temp is string::npos */
temp = s.find(c);  /* temp is 9 */
temp = s.find(c, 10);  /* temp is 19 */
```

8.2.10 The rfind() Functions

The **rfind**() functions work like **find**() functions ('r' means reverse) except that by default they start the search at the end of the invoking string, going in the left direction. So essentially they are trying to find the last occurrence of the given string or character. They have the identical argument signatures as **find**() functions except that the default **pos** value is **string::npos**, indicating that the search begins at the end and going in the left direction.

8.2.11 The erase() Functions

The **erase**() functions allow you to remove a sequence of characters from a string. A commonly used function is described as follows:

```
string & erase(int pos = 0, int n = string::npos);
```

This function simply erases a sequence of characters from index **pos**, inclusively, over **n** characters or until the end of the string, whichever comes first.

Here is one example:

```
string a = "Celeste is not everyone's friends";
a.erase(11, 4);  /* a is "Celeste is everyone's friends" */
```

8.2.12 getline()

The standard input function, **cin**, ignores space, tabs, and newlines. In most cases, you want the invisible characters the user enters to be stored in a string as well. Or you want to get the entire line of data from the input stream or file stream. In these situations, you can use **getline**() functions. Their prototypes look something like this:

```
istream & getline(istream & is, string & s, char delim)
istream & getline(istream & is, string & s)
```

Let's talk about the first function first. The first argument is an **istream** object, which is usually **cin**. It can be an **ifstream**'s object, too. The second argument is usually an empty string because it is where the inputted string is stored. The third argument specifies the delimiter, which is read but *not* stored. The second one works like the first one, except that the delimiter is set to be '\n'. Here are several examples:

```
string s, s2;
getline(cin, s);  /* once you press enter, that is the end of input */
getline(cin, s2, '.');  /* cin even ignores newlines! */
```

A microwave emits a radio frequency of 2.5 gigahertz, which turns into heat immediately when absorbed by food.

CHAPTER 9

Segmentation Fault

A Taiwanese tourist walked to the foreign currency exchange center and asked teller to exchange his US$500 to NT currency.
"Why do I got $15000 when I use $18000 get US$500 2 day befo? You think I speak no good english' and you kan cheat on me?"
"No, sir. This is because of fluctuations." (Does it sound like fxxx you Asians?)
"Fuck you Americans $%#@#$@"

So you see, a segmentation fault in your program is even worse than that in a language—at least they are talking but your program isn't.

9.1 What It Really Is

The bane of most programmers is probably the classic bug "segmentation fault". While it is often elusive and insidious, it is there for a reason and there are ways to avoid it. Technically speaking, a program execution yields segmentation fault when the program violates segment structures by accessing an address it is not supposed to access in the memory address space. So how do we know which segments we are allowed to access and which we are not allowed to access? Of course we do. Suppose we declare an array of 10 integers, our program should not go beyond 9 while accessing an element in the array. Sometimes a program changes the return address of a function call inadvertently or purposely (trying to pull off a buffer-overflow attack, for example); in which case it may get a segmentation fault because the function does not return to the place where it's supposed to return. We will see some of the most common causes of a segmentation fault and discuss how to avoid them.

9.2 General Causes

From my experience, the general causes of a segmentation fault are the following: out-of-bounds access of an array, deletion or freeing of memory that has not been allocated a certain way, and access of data members of a null pointer. Let's look into these causes one by one.

As surprising as it may sound, an out-of-bounds access of an array element doesn't always generate a segmentation fault. The following is a sample program that demonstrates the effects of out-of-bounds element accesses of an integer array and of a vector.

```
#include<iostream>
#include<vector>
using namespace std;

int main(int argc, char** argv){
    int i;
    int input;
    vector<int> v;
    int a[100];
    int version;

    if(argc!=2){
        cout<< "usage: exe <version>\n";
        cout<<"where version is 0 for array and 1 for vector implementation
            \n";
        exit(1);
    }
    version=atoi(argv[1]);
    if(version==0) {
        for(i=0;i<100;i++)
            v.push_back(i);
        cout << "There are a total of 100 elements in the vector.\n";
    }
    else {
        for(i=0;i<100;i++)
            a[i]=i;
        cout << "There are a total of 100 elements in the array.\n";
    }
    cout<<"Please input a number: ";
    cin>>input;
    if(version==0){
        cout<<"The "<<input<<"th item in the vector is: ";
```

```
        cout<<v[input];
    }
    else{
        cout<<"The "<<input<<"'th item in the array is: ";
        cout<<a[input];
    }
    return 0;
}
```

Now try inputting 100, 200, or even 1000 and see what happens. Sometimes out-of-bounds array accesses do not result in a segmentation fault! As mentioned earlier, a segmentation fault occurs due to the segment violation in the memory address space. As long as the address does not reference an illegitimate segment (usually the one used by another process), compiler does not raise a segmentation fault but prints out whatever resides at that address, which mostly likely is garbage. Slightly out-of-bounds addresses may well contain data not referenced by any process, so such array element accesses may not result in a segmentation fault, but accessing addresses significantly distant from the allocated space most likely results in a segmentation fault.

The second general cause is incorrect use of standard library functions that allocate and deallocate memory. For example, here is an example of incorrect use of **delete**:

```
#include<iostream>
using namespace std;

int main(){
    int a=5;
    int *b=&a;
    delete b;
    return 0;
}
```

If you compile and run it, it is likely to give you a segmentation fault because **delete** is used with a pointer that did not use **new** earlier to allocate memory. You cannot apply **delete** to free memory allocated without using **new**. By the way, you do not have to use the same pointer you used with **new**; you just have to use the same address, as the following example illustrates:

```
int *a = new int;  // allocate memory via new
int *b = a;  // b points to the address a points to
delete b;    // perfectly legal
```

The third general cause is trying to access data associated with a null pointer. Suppose you have a pointer pointing to a struct which has a couple of data items. To access those data items, the pointer needs to point to a defined struct object; it cannot be a null pointer or a pointer pointing to an undefined struct reference. In these situations, accesses to data items of the struct most likely result in a segmentation fault. On the other hand, it is possible, though rarely, that after you use **new** to allocate memory and use that memory you get a segmentation fault. This is most likely due to memory shortage. If this is the case, **new** returns the value 0, or NULL. So you can check what is returned by **new** before you start manipulating data of that object.

9.3   How to Avoid It

After my having pointed out the common causes of a segmentation fault, it should be easy to see how to avoid it. First of all, whenever you use an array, make sure you never do anything that will result in the array's going out of bounds. For example, if you expect the array's index from user, you should check that it is within the array's range.

Secondly, whenever you use **free** or **delete** to deallocate memory, always make sure you have used **malloc** (paired with **free**) or **new** (paired with **delete**) earlier to allocate that piece of memory. Other combinations of allocating memory and deallocating memory are either undefined or forbidden, so steer clear of them. Also, do not free memory twice. Let me share with you my experience of using **delete**. I allocate memory for an array, but later depending on the condition in an **if** block, control goes different routes. One of them has the corresponding memory deallocated but the other has it deallocated twice, which results in a segmentation fault. It takes a while to debug, but it'd be nice to pay attention to each possible control flow to begin with.

Finally, before you manipulate a pointer, make sure it points to a valid address. Using **new** is a good idea because it does its best to not give you a segmentation fault no matter how you access data associated with the address pointed to by the pointer. On the other hand, if you don't want to use the pointer at the moment, making it point to NULL is not a bad idea.

Each human eye has about 200 eyelashes, each of which has an average life of 3 to 5 months.

CHAPTER 10

Layout of a Program

It is said that when God created a human being, he was thinking about where head, torso, arms, and legs should go. At first he put head at the bottom and everything else above it, but then the human could not even walk. So he changed the configuration. He put head first, then torso, then legs around torso, then arms below torso.
"Not bad looking at all."
The human could walk in this layout, but not for long. Arms were too slender and weak to support the body for long. Finally he decided that head be at the top position, then torso, then arms around torso, then legs below torso.

Now you should see the importance of sticking to a layout for your programs.

10.1 Typical Layout of a Program

In this chapter we are going to discuss where things are placed in a program. Sometimes some things need to be at specific places in order for the program to compile successfully, but most of the time you can arrange the layout of a program any way you want. It is important to adhere to a layout scheme because doing so removes confusion and speeds up debugging since you are fully aware where things go. Throughout my programming life, I have come to stick to the following layout in a typical program:

Comments about the author, what the program does, etc

Headers

Global variables and objects, initialized or not initialized

Function prototypes (may be omitted)

Function definitions (can also go after main)

```
main {
        All conditions that need to be satisfied to continue*

        All variables and objects declarations, initialized or not initialized

        Initializations of the variables as appropriate

        Main body (appropriate newlines and comments are inserted for clarity)

        return 0;
}
```

*Sometimes the command line inputted by the user does not fulfill the requirements necessary for the program to run. In that case, print an error message (and a message telling the user how to use the program) and exit.

Let's look at each component of the layout. First, you include comments about the author and what the program does, how to run it, and so on. Then you include the necessary headers that provide functions your program needs. If you need to include a library that is less often used, it is advisable for you to also include a comment indicating what functions it provides will be used. Next, you declare all the global variables. Sometimes you want to assign values to the global variables but other times you do it inside **main**() or other functions. Also, if you want to declare an object of a particular class to be global, you can do it here. Next you put function prototypes, but they are not necessary for the program to compile as long as you always call a function after you define it. Next, put function definitions. You can put them before **main**() or after **main**(). I like to put them after **main**() so that it's easier for me to debug later. What comes next is our favorite function—**main**(). In the argument of **main**(), you may want to include (**int argc, char **argv**) to receive data from the command line. Inside **main**(), before you declare your variables, sometimes you want to check to see if the user has given correct information for the program to run. This happens a lot because many programs have different variations depending on the given parameters. The results of running a program, thus, depend on what the user inputs. It is generally easier to receive all data from command line once and for all. After the program receives valid data, it can go ahead and declare and initialize variables. Many programmers tend to declare variables immediately before they are needed to limit their scopes, and that's not a bad idea. Next, I initialize those variables as I see fit. In some situations I assign values to them right before I use them. If I declare a pointer which I don't use at the moment, I always assign it to NULL. Coming next is the body of **main**(). As you type along, you may want to insert comments and newlines as appropriate for clarity and readability of the program. Here is a sample program following the above layout:

```
/*
Michael Wen
7/1/2003
This program, given the number of sides, produces code for Matlab to display
a regular polygon of specified number of sides onscreen.
*/
#include<iostream>
#include<math.h>                /*for acos()*/
#include<vector>
#include<fstream>
using namespace std;

const double PI = acos(-1.0); /*value of pi*/
vector<double> x;
vector<double> y;
const double length=4.9;
const double offset=length/2;
const double unit=offset*0.81;
char *file;
ofstream fout;

int main(int argc, char** argv){
    if(argc!=3){
        cout<<"usage: exe <num> <file>\n";
        cout<<"<num>: number of sides\n";
        cout<<"<file>: output file's name\n";
        exit(1);
    }
    int num, i;
    double degree, transition;
    num=atoi(argv[1]);
    file=argv[2];
    degree=transition=0;
    transition=360.0/num;

    for(i=0;i<num;i++){
```

```
        x.push_back(unit*cos(degree*PI/180)+offset);
        y.push_back(unit*sin(degree*PI/180)+offset);
        degree+=transition;
    }
    fout.open(file);
    fout<<"axis([0 "<<offset*2<<" 0 "<<offset*2<<"]);\n";
    fout<<"x=[";
    for(i=0;i<x.size();i++)
        fout<<x[i]<<' ';
    fout<<x[0]<<"];\n";
    fout<<"y=[";
    for(i=0;i<y.size();i++)
        fout<<y[i]<<' ';
    fout<<y[0]<<"];\n";
    fout<<"line(x,y);\n";
    fout.close();
    return 0;
}
```

Our sun can hold about one million Earths.

CHAPTER 11

A Model for Writing a Program

Before Alexander Blue became one of the world's most famous architects, every house he built ended up collapsing in smithereens. He always plunged right into building the house without thinking too much. One day Savior came along and said to him, "You can't get started until you grok it." With that he left.

After several days of meditation on Sahara Desert, Blue looked down bluely at the scribble he made with his feet on the sand and a thought suddenly struck him. "O yea, why don't I put my ideas down on paper before I build the house?"

From then on every house he built became a popular resort and millions of visitors swarmed the place every year. In fact, the word "blueprint" is coined in honor of him. Whom did he have to thank for?

Therefore, why not follow suit and put your ideas down on paper before you write your programs so that one day you will become a world-famous programmer?

11.1 Characteristics of a Good Program

Below we will discuss characteristics of a good program, including short code size, high efficiency, and high reliability.

11.2 Code Size

Code size refers to the number of lines of a program. In general, the lower the code size, the higher a program's readability and efficiency, but it is not always the case. For example, we discussed in Chapter 4 two types of functions that compute a Fibonacci number: recursive version and non-recursive version. The recursive version takes fewer lines of code than the non-recursive version; however, the time complexity of the recursive version is way out of sight.

There are several ways to reduce the code size of a program. One of the most effective ways is to understand the programming language thoroughly. For example, the following statement, assuming a, b, c are initialized integers:

```
a = b < c ? 10 : 20;
```

is equivalent to

```
if (b < c)
      a = 10;
else
      a = 20;
```

But if you do not know how ?: works, you cannot make this optimization. There are plenty of other examples that illustrate the fact that knowing a language well can help you reduce code size. Here is another one. The following statement:

```
for_each(lottery.begin(), lottery.end(), drawLottery);
```

can replace

```
vector<int>::iterator vi;
for(vi = lottery.begin(); vi != lottery.end(); vi++)
      drawLottery(*vi);
```

There are many functions provided by C++ standard libraries that you can use to your advantage. You need to explore more in order to get a decent grasp of C++ libraries. By simply including the libraries in the header and calling appropriate functions in the body, you can reduce code size dramatically. In addition, most functions in the standard library have gone through exhaustive testing and optimizing, so they are very robust and error-resilient. If something goes wrong, they generally won't make your program crash.

Other ways to reduce code size include reducing the number of functions, using fewer variables and data objects, figuring out a different technique to tackle the same problem, and so on. An example of using a different technique is using a formula to calculate the sum of successive squares of integers $(1^2+2^2+3^2+\ldots+n^2)$ as opposed to doing it the hard way.

11.3 Efficiency

Efficiency refers to the running time of a program. Clearly, the faster the program runs, the better. It usually takes technical knowledge to achieve great efficiency, especially in advanced data structures. For instance, a binary search tree generally offers greater efficiency than a linear search mechanism such as an array; however, in its worst cases, its efficiency is no better than the linear method. Experienced programmers may choose to use another data structure such as a balanced binary search tree (e.g. AVL tree) despite its rather complicated design. Many data structures have been designed and implemented over the past few decades, and each of them has its advantages and disadvantages.

The design of a program also has a significant impact on its efficiency. It includes the means to store data, the techniques to solve a subtask, the program's flow control, and so on. Proficiency comes with experience and explorations.

Another way to increase efficiency of a program is to be familiar with C++ standard library. If you know exactly how its functions are implemented, you know their time complexities. For example, the containers provided by STL have many operations in common, but they have different time complexities. The **deque** template class supports insertion and removal of data items in constant time, whereas **vector** takes linear time. If you are familiar with their implementations, then when it comes time to determining which functions or techniques to use, you will be able to make wise decisions.

As you can see, achieving maximum efficiency of a program basically means you have to know the language extremely well, which may take a decade. Many programmers are not too much concerned with the efficiency of a program because they think as long as it works and does not take ridiculously long, it's fine. However, if you write a program that handles a large set of data, you will notice the significance of data structure and program design, and thus realize the importance of efficiency.

11.4 Reliability

Ideally, your program should never crash no matter what the user inputs. Even if the user enters invalid data, your program should handle it appropriately. The worse thing it can do is to terminate the program. At times this is hard to achieve; for instance, you expect the user to give a file according to a specific format. If file is completely out of accordance with that format, how do you process that file? One way to do this is to check the validity of the file before you process it; if the file is improperly formatted, output an error message and terminate the program. Another way is to check while processing it. To sum up, it is dismaying for a user who accidentally enters the wrong inputs to see the program crash immediately. Whenever you write a program, think about how well your program reacts to the most deranged psychotic in the world.

11.5   Understand What You Need to Do

Anybody with programming experience most likely agrees that everything has a tough beginning. In programming, you must be able to rid yourself of any doubts before you can start. If you have doubts about the objective or implementation of an assigned program, bring them up to your instructor, teaching assistant, or even friends. Make sure you absolutely understand what you need to do in the program. I have the experience that I misunderstood a small part of a program I was writing and ended up earning only half of the credit. Even if I did detect this little misunderstanding before I turned the assignment in, chances are that I needed to pull major changes in my program and I wouldn't be able to make it. Therefore, knowing what the program needs to do is the first task at hand.

11.6   Working from Scratch—with a Computer Versus on Paper

Many programmers love to start typing their programs on a computer without giving it much thought, including myself when I was a freshman in college. Writing programs this way generally yields poor results. Without a clear idea of how to implement the program, things can hardly go well. Shortly later I found that working on paper first would yield much better results. I write out rough guidelines and pseudo-code, and think about how to implement each part of the program. Once I figure the whole thing out, I begin coding on a computer. In the next section we will talk about what to write on paper so that you'll understand why working on paper first is much better than working on a computer.

11.7 A Four-Step Model

You are probably not convinced how working on paper makes it easier to write a program, but there are several things you should do before you plunge into coding. I devised these steps and they have helped me finish every single programming assignment since then. Here are the four steps of developing a program that I adopt:

Step 1: write a skeleton of the program
Step 2: write a summary of variables and refine the skeleton of the program as necessary
Step 3: determine interrelations, states, and scopes of variables
Step 4: code, test, and optimize; go back to any previous step as necessary

The *first* step says that you need to write a pseudo-code of the program so that you know what needs to be done at what point in the program. Before you do that you should think about the program and get some idea first. Don't forget to think about preconditions and postconditions of each function, if any.

The *second* step tells you that you need to identify variables (including objects of classes and user-defined types) you will be using to store data. While doing this, you may want to refine the skeleton you made during step 1.

The *third* step suggests that you need to hone the definitions of variables and to draw relations among them. They are usually independent of one another, but in large programs, they can be highly dependent upon each other; modifying one's value affects others' results. You need to inspect each variable carefully so that you know if modifying a variable creates desired effects. On the other hand, you need to be clear on the states of variables at any point while the program is running. For example, let's say you are using a string array to store all words of a dictionary. At some point you may need to modify the array in order to acquire some critical information, later you may want to restore it in its previous state. Programmers can be careless about the states of variables until major bugs hit them. Whenever you intend to manipulate a variable, make sure its contents are what you expect. Another example is whenever you use a loop, make sure that at the start of each iteration you assign desired values to variables used in the loop. For instance, you may need to assign 0 to a variable at the start of every iteration so that at the end of each iteration you get desired value stored in the variable. Lastly, you want to give each variable an appropriate scope. Most of you probably think that avoiding using global variables is the best policy. However, in a program full of data dependencies, consider giving global scope to the variables that many of functions need so that you don't need to pass them around in function parameters. As you grow experienced, you will see more clearly what variable deserves which scope. When you are done with step 3, you should be able to visualize how the program works and be confident that your program will eventually be completed. If not, keep working on this step or return to earlier steps because if you jump to step 4 without having a proper design of the program, chances are that things go wrong at some point and you end up having to perform major changes. To sum up, you need to be clear on the following things:

- interrelations among variables
- state of each variable
- scope of each variable

Of course not every variable deserves such critical attention. As you become more experienced you will know how each variable should be handled. This step is a *very, very* crucial step in making your program work.

Step 4, the final step, is self-explanatory. You begin coding on a computer according to the skeleton you have devised. Make sure you include necessary headers. Along the way, you may want to test the completed part to make sure you are on the right track. A common dangerous thing a programmer does is to write everything out, then debug. This practice usually works with small programs, but trust me, once you get your hands on a larger program, individual unit testing becomes imperative. In addition, after the program is done, you may want to see if you can apply any optimization to it so that it is shorter, more readable, and more efficient. We will see a couple of examples later.

11.8   Divide and Conquer

In terms of programming techniques, divide and conquer is a common way to design algorithms. It essentially consists of two steps:

Divide: Divide a big problem into smaller ones, then solve them recursively until they hit the base case, which you use brute force to solve.
Conquer: The solution to the initial problem comes from the solutions to its subproblems.

However, what I mean here is to divide the program into a group of tasks and deal with them one by one. When code that does one task is written, particularly a function, you should go ahead and test it to see if it fully works, hence conquering a part of the program. When testing it, you should take into account every possible precondition and postcondition associated with that function. This is part of the fourth step we discussed in the previous section.

11.9   Practice #1

You need to write a program to output a ruler's calibration. You cannot simply output the results using **cout**; otherwise there won't be any fun and frustration. The program must output the following:

After you examine the output, you should have some idea how to implement the program. Apply the four steps and see if you are up for the challenge. The following is the results of my following the four steps:

Step 1: A close inspection tells us that a loop can accomplish this job by first outputting a | in the leftmost and rightmost positions, then calculating the distance from leftmost point to the middle point for next iteration, which is half the distance between the two |'s. Once we have the distance, for every amount of that distance starting at the leftmost point, we output a |. In the next iteration, we find the distance between one | and the next |, cut it in half, and output a | for every amount of that distance starting at the leftmost point. This process goes on until the distance becomes 1, which we have reached the bottom. Having this in mind, Let's go ahead and apply the first step. It requires us to draft a skeleton of the program, which should look something like this:

```
int main(){
-declare a char array and fill it with space, don't forget to terminate it with '\0'
-obtain distance between leftmost and rightmost positions of the ruler; in this
case, it should be 0 + 32, or 32.
```

-use a loop; while the distance is greater than zero, the following happens:
 fill the array with | at each multiple of the distance
 output that array
 update distance by dividing it by two
}

Step 2: Let's decide what variables and objects we need to store data. As the skeleton suggests, we need a **char** array, an index for the **for** loop, and an **int** for distance. So here it goes:

```
int main(){
        char ruler[33];
        int i,dist;
```

-declare a char array and fill it with space, don't forget to terminate it with '\0'
-obtain distance between leftmost and rightmost positions of the ruler; in this case, it should be 0 + 32, or 32.
-use a loop; while the distance is greater than zero, the following happens:
 fill the array with | at each multiple of the distance
 output that array
 update distance by dividing it by two
}

Step 3: Here is a breakdown of this step and the corresponding observations:
Interrelation: Whenever **ruler** uses **i** as the index of a loop, **i** can never go out of **ruler**'s bounds. When **i** is used as a distance increment, make sure it gets the right value.
State: **ruler** should be filled with spaces initially, then contain increasingly more |'s until it contains nothing but |. **i** may be used for indexing more than once, so make sure whenever you start using it, it is set to the beginning of the array. **dist** should be 32 initially and cut in half in each round of printing the ruler.
Scope: All variables can stay local.

Step 4: Here is the complete program, including as comments the above skeleton:

```
#include<iostream>
using namespace std;

int main(){
        char ruler[33];
```

```
    int i,dist;

/*
declare a char array and fill it in with space
*/
    for(i=1;i<33;i++)
        ruler[i]=' ';
/*
obtain distance between leftmost and rightmost positions of the ruler; in this
case, it should be 0 + 32, or 32.
*/
    dist=32;
    while(dist>0){
/*
fill the array with | at each multiple of the distance
*/
        for(i=0;i<33;i+=dist)
            ruler[i]='|';
/* output that array */
        cout<<ruler<<endl;
/* update distance by dividing it by two */
        dist/=2;
    }
    return 0;
}
```

This program uses a **char** array, but you don't have to use an array; you can simply calculate the appropriate distance and use **cout** to output a | or a space. These four steps work for me, and they should work for you too. Make sure you practice often so that you can begin to program *finitely*, the sole purpose of reading this book.

500 years after you dispose of an aluminum can, it still exists.

CHAPTER 12

A Model for Writing a Function

Same joke as the one presented in Chapter 11.

12.1 Characteristics of a Good Function

Below we will discuss several characteristics of a good function, including short code size, high efficiency, and high generality.

12.2 Code Size

As discussed in the previous chapter, small code size is generally better for a program. It is true for a function, too. A function with big code size can be hard to read and to understand. However, when efficiency issues are taken into account, code size is no longer as important. As discussed several times, the recursive function to calculate a Fibonacci number is low in code size but is extremely inefficient. In this situation, the non-recursive version is much favored.

12.3 Efficiency

Efficiency refers to the time complexity of a function. If two functions achieve the same purpose but one is significantly faster, it is always more desired. Efficiency can hurt code size and code size can hurt efficiency; it's crucial to find a balance between them.

12.4 Generality

How general is your function? Is the function written to deal with one specific situation or many? A program with many functions can become difficult to understand. For example, if a program needs to deal with five different requests issued by a user, it can call five distinct functions each of which takes care of one request. This example has been discussed in <u>Section 4.5</u>. However, it can also call one function, given the identity of the request. The latter way is generally more desired because it is possible that there are overlapping operations among some of the requests. Sometimes when the subtasks for your program are too different, you may not be able to generalize them in just a few functions. In that situation, you still can try to find a set of common operations that many tasks need, then write one function to do that, which can be used by as many tasks as necessary.

Also, a function that performs a general task (e.g. converting a **double** to a C++ string) may be highly reusable. A function that performs too specialized a task is low on reusability.

In addition, a function template is a good option to provide generality: One function works with multiple argument types. However, opportunities of using function templates don't come about often.

12.5 Understand What the Function Should Do

The first and foremost thing you need to do is to understand *exactly* what the function should do. Writing a function takes precision and caution because the preconditions and postconditions must be determined in advance and be preserved all along. We will discuss preconditions and postconditions in more detail in the next section.

12.6 Preconditions and Postconditions

We briefly discussed this topic in <u>Section 4.1</u>; let's take a closer look at it in this chapter. Preconditions refer to the states of variables before the program calls the function, including restrictions on its arguments, if any. Postconditions refer to the states of variables after the program calls the function, including what the function returns. If the function modifies a global variable, for example, this variable's state should be included in the preconditions. A tremendous number of bugs occur due to incomplete understanding of preconditions and postconditions of a function. For instance, if you pass a negative integer to a function that handles only positive integers, you get weird results or even a segmentation fault. Another example is that if the result of calling a function is further processed by the program, you need to make sure the program can deal with every single possible result the function returns. That is why if you do not pay enough attention to a function's preconditions and postconditions, it is highly possible that your function works on some arguments and crashes on others. Therefore, when you write a function, always include preconditions and postconditions inside comments right above the function as a reminder.

12.7 A Four-Step Model

Just like writing a program, writing a function should be done on paper and coded on a computer. The four steps of writing a function is:

Step 1: write a skeleton of the function, including determining preconditions and postconditions
Step 2: write a summary of variables and refine the skeleton of the function as necessary
Step 3: determine interrelations and states of variables
Step 4: code, test, and optimize; go back to any previous step as necessary

Having worked through the previous chapter, you shouldn't have difficulty understanding the requirements of each step. One thing to note is that we no longer need to worry about scopes of variables because each variable to be used is declared inside the function. As we all know, the design of a function is critical to writing a good function. Step 4 follows the design step 1 through 3 develop, so don't hurry through them. If while coding you realize that a much better design exists and you decide to use that design, you will need to go back to step 1 and some of your work, if not all, goes down the drain. The key to judging whether a function design is sound is to go through it carefully, asking yourself whether you really need to do the current subtask. You will get better and better at this if you do this every time you write a function. After you complete step 2, you are encouraged to go through the skeleton with a sample set of arguments in mind. Careful review could reveal hidden errors and potential bugs.

12.8 Practice #1

Let's write a function that parses a string. Let's say the string contains data items that are separated by '#'s and the last item also has a '#' appended to it. For example, "selena#is#a#nice#girl#but#fate#kicks#her#in#the#teeth#" is a valid string. Here are the function's specifications:

- The function takes as argument a **string** to be parsed and an **int** specifying which substring to return, starting at 1.
- The function returns a **string** which is either the target or an empty string if the target is not found.
- A **for** loop and several **if-else** statements should suffice.

For example, if the string to be parsed is "long#time#no#see#Dali#and#Yuchien#" and the string we want is the 5th one, then the function should return "Dali".

Again, try to write the program by yourself. Don't be frustrated if you meet obstacles; try to leap over them. Practice makes perfect.

Step 1: Let's first determine the preconditions and postconditions of the function. The first argument is a **string**, and the second one is an integer. If the first argument is not a valid **string**, the function may not return the correct result. If the second argument is negative or is too big, the function should return an empty string. Keep in mind that segmentation fault is not an option. Let's write down the preconditions and postconditions in a more formal way:

Precondition: The first argument is a **string**; the second argument is an **int**.
Postcondition: If the first argument is not a valid **string**, the function may not return the correct result. If the second argument is negative or is too big, the function should return an empty **string**.

Now let's draft a skeleton of the function. What the function does is straightforward and should not confuse you. Here is a skeleton I came up with:

```
/*
precondition: s contains data, delimited by '#'; n is the position of the data
desired
postcondition: returns the desired data; if error occurs, return an empty string
*/
string parse(string s, int i) {
- use a for loop to scan every single character in s
- do the following inside the for loop
      do nothing until the (i-1)'th # is reached, which signals the start of the
      target
      start collecting the characters until the next # or the end of string is reached
- return the string just collected
```

- if no string is collected, return an empty string
}

Step 2: As you can see, we need a **string** to keep track of the target we need to return; we need a counter that counts the number of #'s so that we know when we need to start collecting data; we also need as many indices as the number of **for** loops. Here is the modified skeleton:

```
/*
precondition: s contains data, delimited by '#'; n is the position of the data
desired
postcondition: returns the desired data; if error occurs, return an empty string
*/
string parse(string s, int i) {
    int i, j;
    string t="";
    int counter=0;
```

- use a for loop to scan every single character in s
- do the following inside the for loop
    do nothing until the (i-1)th # is reached, which signals the start of the target
    use a for loop to collect the characters until the next # or the end of string is
    reached
- return the string just collected
- if no string is collected, return an empty string
}

As you can see, I modified the skeleton slightly and now I need to use two for loops.

Step 3:
Interrelation: If **s** uses index **i** or **j** to access a character of the **string**, the index cannot be outside its bounds.
State: **i** and **j** are indices for the two for loops, and you should use one in the first **for** loop and the other in the other **for** loop. This is also a common source of bugs—reusing a variable when you are not supposed to. Beginner programmers may use the same variable for indexing both for loops and the program produces mysterious results. On the other hand, **t** should contain the target **string** right before its content is returned, and **counter** should point to the correct data item before **t** can start collecting.

Step 4: Now let's code it. After you write your own version, compare it with mine, which looks like:

```
#include<iostream>
#include<string>    /* or <string.h> */
using namespace std;
/*
precondition: s contains data, delimited by '#'; n is the position of the data
desired
postcondition: returns the desired data; if error occurs, return an empty string
*/
string parse(string s, int n) {
     int i, j;
     string t="";
     int counter=0;

/* use a for loop to scan every single character in s */
     for(i=0;i<s.length();i++) {
          if(s[i]=='#')          /* do nothing until the (i-1)th # is reached */
               counter++;
          if(counter==n-1) {
/* collect the characters until the next # or the end of string is reached */
               for(j=i+1;j<s.length();j++) {
                    if(s[j]=='#')
                         return t;   /* return the string just collected */
                    t+=s[j];
               }
          }
     }
     return ""; /* if no string is collected, return an empty string */
}
```

Everything looks good. If you run this function to test it, however, you will realize that there is a tiny bug in it. This function works with **n** bigger than or equal to two; it misses the first character of the target when **n** is one. Debugging is part of step 4, so let's focus on why the function does not work properly when **n** is one. After carefully inspecting the code, you should realize that the second **for** loop starts at index i+1, and when **n** is one, it skips the first character; when **n** is two or bigger, it skips '#'. Now that we've pinned down the bug, we should get rid of it.

One solution is to treat it as a special case: test to see if **n** is 1 before program enters the first **for** loop; if so, start collecting data and return it; if not, enter the **for** loop. Treating exceptions as special cases is often practiced, but it requires more code, making the function inelegant. Let's try to come up with a cleaner way to fix this bug.

What about switching the two **if** blocks inside the first **for** loop? That way we just start collecting characters once we are at the right place! A slight modification to the function yields the following:

```cpp
#include<iostream>
#include<string>    /* or <string.h> */
using namespace std;
/*
precondition: s contains data, delimited by '#'; n is the position of the data desired
postcondition: returns the desired data; if error occurs, return an empty string
*/
string parse(string s, int n) {
    int i, j;
    string t="";
    int counter=0;

/* use a for loop to scan every single character in s */
    for(i=0;i<s.length();i++) {
        if(counter==n-1) {
/* collect the characters until the next # or the end of string is reached */
            for(j=i;j<s.length();j++) {
                if(s[j]=='#')
                    return t;   /* return the string just collected */
                t+=s[j];
            }
        }
        if(s[i]=='#') /* do nothing until the (i-1)th # is reached */
            counter++;
    }
    return "";  /* if no string is collected, return an empty string */
}
```

After examining the code mentally, you shouldn't have any problem seeing how the bug is removed. This version works perfectly and always preserves preconditions. In addition, it never gives a segmentation fault no matter what the arguments are.

12.9   Practice #2

Let's practice writing another useful function from scratch. In java, the utility package supports a nifty class called **StringTokenizer**, but there is no such class in C++. Many have come up with their own version of tokenizing a **string**. Let's see if we are able to write a function to do this task.

Your version of the string tokenizer receives a **string** which contains data separated by user-defined delimiters (usually a space), then retrieves individual data items, also known as tokens. Here is one possible prototype of the function:

vector<string> tokenize(string s);

Here is a list of specifications of this function:
- The function returns a **vector<string>** that stores all tokens of s.
- Delimiters include all unprintable characters.
- Make sure none of the tokens contains any unprintable characters.

Let's write down the preconditions and postconditions in a formal way:
precondition: s contains tokens separated by unprintable characters
postcondition: returns a **vector** that contains all tokens

Step 1: First we need to come up with a skeleton of the function. Mine looks like:

```
/*
precondition: s contains tokens separated by unprintable characters
postcondition: returns a vector that contains all tokens of s
*/
vector<string> tokenize(string s){
- eliminate spaces and tabs before and after s, if any
- do the following inside the while loop
        take all characters until an unprintable character is reached
        store it in the vector
        skip all unprintable characters until a printable character is reached
```

- return the vector
}

Step 2: We need a **vector<string>** to store the tokens; we probably need one or more indexing variables inside our loops. Now let's incorporate variables into our skeleton:

```
/*
precondition: s contains tokens separated by unprintable characters
postcondition: returns a vector that contains all tokens of s
*/
vector<string> tokenize(string s){
    int i, j;
    vector<string> vs;
```

- eliminate spaces and tabs before and after s, if any
- do the following inside the while loop
    take all characters until an unprintable character is reached
    store it in the vector
    skip all unprintable characters until a printable character is reached
- return the vector
}

Step 3:
<u>Interrelation</u>: If **i** or **j** is used as index for **vs**, it cannot go out of its bounds.
<u>State</u>: As the program runs, **vs** will contain more and more tokens.

Step 4: To test if a character is printable, use **isgraph()** defined in <cctype>. It takes a **char** argument and returns true if it is a printing character. The library's **isprint()** is similar but it returns true if the argument is a space. This is a live example of reducing code size we discussed earlier this chapter. If you do not use **isgraph()**, you will need to take care of all unprintable characters by yourself. It is important that you code this function by yourself for practice. After you are done, take a look at my version.

```
/*
precondition: s contains tokens separated by unprintable characters
postcondition: returns a vector that contains all tokens of s
*/
vector<string> tokenize(string s){
```

```
        int i,j;
        vector<string> vs;
        int slen=s.length();

        j=-1;
/* eliminate spaces and tabs before and after s, if any */
        while(!isgraph(s[++j]) && j<slen)
                ;
        s=s.substr(j);
        j=s.length();
        while(!isgraph(s[--j]) && j>=0)
                ;
        s=s.substr(0,j+1);

/* append a space in the end of temp for next while loop */
        s+=' ';

        i=j=0;
        while(j<s.length()){
/* take all characters until an unprintable character is reached */
                while(isgraph(s[++j]) && j<slen)
                        ;
/* store it in the vector */
                vs.push_back(s.substr(i,j-i));
/* skip all unprintable characters until a printable character is reached */
                while(!isgraph(s[++j]) && j<slen)
                        ;
                i=j;
        }
/* return the vector */
        return vs;
}
```

I use <string>'s **substr()** in this function. You can refer to Section 8.2.2 to learn how to use it. The most annoying thing about writing this function is determining the index of a character in s and the arguments of **substr()**, which takes a little finesse. Let me explain how this function works. I assign −1 to **j** because in the while loop the index is **++j**, which increments **j** first before it is used. That done, the following line s=s.substr(j);

Copies a substring from index j because s[j] is a printable character. The next sub-task is to get rid of trailing unprintable characters. You shouldn't have any problem seeing how it works. The next **while** loop is the heart of the function; it retrieves all tokens and stores them in a **vector<string>** object. I use the same logic to get rid of unprintable characters. The reason that I need to append a space to **s** before entering the **while** loop is that when skipping all unprintable characters until a printable character is reached, I increment **j** first. Without a space after the last token, this action will result in an array out-of-bound access.

After several test runs, we see that the function works perfectly. You may feel that the function is a bit too long and there is redundant code. Let's look at our design again. Why do we need to get rid of unprintable characters first? Can't we simply enter a **while** loop which skips unprintable characters and stores a sequence of printable characters in each iteration?

Yes, that's exactly what I meant when I said, *"design of a function is critical to writing a good function."* Now that a better design hits us, we can choose whether to use the old design or the new one. Bear in mind, though, that the bigger the program, the more time it takes to redo it. Since this function is rather small, let's practice more by building our function on the new design. Here is our new skeleton, including variables:

```
/*
precondition: s contains tokens separated by unprintable characters
postcondition: returns a vector that contains all tokens of s
*/
vector<string> tokenize(string s){
    int i, j;
    vector<string> vs;

- use a while loop to retrieve all tokens
- do the following inside the while loop until all characters of s are scanned
    skip all unprintable characters until a printable character is reached
    take all characters until an unprintable character is reached
    store it in the vector
- return the vector
}
```

Let's go ahead and code it. Here is my code:

```
/*
precondition: s contains tokens separated by unprintable characters
postcondition: returns a vector that contains all tokens of s
*/
vector<string> tokenize(string s){
    int i,j;
    vector<string> vs;
    int slen=s.length();

    j=0;
/* use a while loop to retrieve all tokens */
    while(j<slen){
/* skip all unprintable characters until a printable character is reached */
        while(!isgraph(s[j++]) && j<slen)
            ;
        if(j>=slen) return vs;
        i=j-1;
/* take all characters until an unprintable character is reached */
        while(isgraph(s[j++]) && j<slen)
            ;
/* store it in the vector */
        if(j>=slen) j++;
        vs.push_back(s.substr(i,j-i-1));
    }
/* return the vector */
    return vs;
}
```

After testing it several times, we are certain that it works perfectly. As we can see, this version looks shorter and cleaner than the previous one. It is also more efficient. If we had been dealing with a much larger program, we would have had to spend a lot more time redesigning and recoding. Therefore, you should think more carefully while designing the skeleton of your program. Try to stick to the cleanest and most efficient design.

A lion can sleep up to 20 hours a day.

CHAPTER 13

Documentation

"Sorry about losing the case," apologizes Bloodsucker.
"Well we would've stood a much better chance if you had documented our case."
Bloodsucker got paid nothing, and since the case is not documented at all he cannot
sue his client: He can't even prove he had worked on that case. What a loser.

So you see, it's important to document your program lest you love being a loser.

13.1 Its Importance

Everybody should know that detailed documentation in a program is very important because it explains every stage of the program and how it achieves a particular task. Only good documentation can serve these purposes; poor
documentation lacks clarifications and makes programs even less readable. Some
think documenting a program takes too much time and is not necessary because
experienced programmers should be able to decipher the meaning of each line of
code. While this is true in most cases, it is not in others. In big, complex programs, certain variables are used indirectly to do complicated operations.
Without seeing any comments, a programmer could be totally clueless. Giving
meaningful names to variables and other program elements helps a lot, and com-
plementing it with comments is even better. Getting into the habit of documenting every program you write will prove beneficial to you and people who read
your programs.

13.2 Danger in using /* */

As I become more experienced in programming, I realize that there is a subtle
danger in using /* */ to comment their programs: nested pairs cause problems.
Try putting /*, /*, */, */, in your code in this order and see if the program can still
be compiled. The fact is that the first */ blocks everything and leaves whatever

after it open for compiling. For example, the following is a program fragment with nested pairs of /* and */:

```
/*
This program simulates a calculator.
        /*
        The calculator's functions include addition, subtraction, multiplica-
tion,
        division, and modulus.
        */
by Michael Wen
*/

int main() {
...
    return 0;
}
```

The seventh line, "by Michael Wen", is not commented out and is visible to the compiler. Therefore compiling this program will not be successful. Programmers usually do not use nested comments anyway, but what if you to compile a specific portion of the code and leave the other portion as comments within which there are several pairs of /* and */? Here is a wonderful solution: you can use **define** pre-processor directives. Here are two examples, A and B:

```
A:
#ifdefine whatever
Following is code I do NOT want compiled
.
.
.
/*
comments...
*/
Following is code I do NOT want compiled
.
.
.
/*
more comments...
```

```
*/.
Following is code I do NOT want compiled
.
.
.
#endif

B:
#ifndefine whatever
Following is code I do want compiled
.
.
.
/*
comments...
*/
Following is code I do want compiled
.
.
.
/*
more comments...
*/.
Following is code I do want compiled
.
.
.
#endif
```

If **whatever** is defined, compiler compiles everything after **#ifdefine whatever** and before the corresponding **#endif**. If **whatever** is defined, compiler does not compile anything after **#ifndefine** whatever and before the corresponding **#endif**. In example A, the entire code after **#ifdefine whatever** and before **#endif** is not compiled. In example B, the entire code after **#ifndefine whatever** and before **#endif** is compiled. Simply inserting and removing the letter 'n' in the **define** directive makes life a lot easier if you want or do not want something compiled.

13.3 Danger in using //

In my first year of programming, I always used // to comment my program because I thought it was a more convenient way than using /* and */. As time went on, I realized that /* and */ are a lot better for the following reasons:

- They can enclose lines after lines of comments.
- They usually improve readability of a program.
- You can be sure that whatever between /* and */ always stays as comments whatever platform to which you transport your code.

The final reason is the main reason. I use Microsoft Notepad to code, and after I am done I send it to my computer science account for compiling or other purposes. I've found that when I display my code in a text editor, sometimes comments after // are wrapped into multiple lines and the subsequent lines are not seen as comments any more. To correct the problem, I need to make them comments again by either adding more // or by adding /* and */. From then on, I started to adopt /* and */. This way I am rest assured that whatever meant to be comments always stay as comments wherever my code is transported.

The back of the refrigerator is painted black because black radiates heat more quickly.

CHAPTER 14

Can You Spot Errors?

14.1 Case 1—type cast

Predict the output of the following program.

```
#include<iostream>
using namespace std;
int main() {
    double result;
    int numOfPies, numOfPeople;
    numOfPies = 14;
    numOfPeople = 3;
    result = numOfPies/numOfPeople;
    cout<<numOfPies<<" pies split up evenly between "<<numOfPeople<<
        " people.\n";
    cout<<"Therefore, each person gets "<<result<<" pies.\n";
    return 0;
}
```

Solution: The output looks like this:

```
14 pies split up evenly between 3 people.
Therefore, each person gets 4 pies.
```

The intention of this program is to divide 14 pies evenly between 3 people, so each one should get 4 2/3 pies, but why does the output say each person gets only 4 pies? First we check the type of **result**, which is **double**, so there should not be any problem. However, **numOfPies** and **numOfPeople** are **int**. The result of **numOfPies/numOfPeople**, therefore, is 4. Now because the types of both operands should match, 4 is transformed into **double**. By examining this example, it is not hard to see that many bugs come from lack of understanding of syntax of the programming language. Therefore, the first step to improve your programming skills is to completely understand the programming language you are using.

14.2 Case 2—cin.get()

The following program is supposed to receive two characters from user, but contains a subtle bug. Point it out and correct it.

```
#include<iostream>
using namespace std;

int main(int argc, char* argv[]) {
    int i;
    char c,c2;
    cout<<"Please enter your favorite character: ";
    cin.get(c);
    cout<<"Please enter your second favorite character: ";
    cin.get(c2);
    cout<<"The first character you entered is "<<c;
    cout<<", and the second one is "<<c2<<endl;
}
```

Solution: The bug results from incorrect use of **get()**. First of all, we need to be totally certain about what **get()** does. It reads a character the user types, *including* a newline. However, it does not respond until user hits **enter**. This is the problem. When user types, for example, "a", then hits **enter**, the second **get()** will get that newline. Therefore, to fix the problem, add another **get()** right after the first **get()**. You can also concatenate **get()** as in "cin.get(c).get();". This situation also exemplifies lack of understanding of the programming language. Someone who just learns **get()** is likely to think that a newline is not covered by **get()**, but he is wrong.

14.3 Case 3—while loop

Predict the output of executing the following program.

```
#include<iostream>
using namespace std;
```

```
#include<string>
int buggy(string s){
    int counter=-1;
    while(counter<s.length())
        counter++;
    return counter;
}
int main(){
    string s = "Charlotte and Marlene are angels.";
    cout<<buggy(s)<<endl;
    return 0;
}
```

Solution: To our surprise, the output is −1, not the length of **s**! However, if you change the initial value of **counter** from −1 to 0, the output will be 33. In fact, the result of evaluating counter<s.length() is false, even though **s.length()** is 33. If you do,

```
int ti=s.length();
cout<<(counter<ti)<<endl;
```

You will get "true". So what is going on here? The problem is that s.length() returns an **unsigned** integer. When compared with an **unsigned** integer, the integer gets promoted to be unsigned. You should be able to figure out the rest; if not refer to Section 16.4.

14.4 Case 4—decimal number

Predict the output of the executing the following program. Pay attention to the very concept of how machines deal with a decimal number.

```
#include<iostream>
using namespace std;
int main(){
    int shape;
    double degree,transition;
    shape=17;
    transition=100.0/shape;
    degree=0;
```

```
    while(true){
        if(degree>100.0){
            cout<<degree<<" is greater than 100.0\n";
            break;
        }
        else if(degree<100.0)
            cout<<degree<<" is smaller than 100.0\n";
        else
            cout<<degree<<" is equal to 100.0\n";
        degree+=transition;
    }
    return 0;
}
```

Solution: Here is the output of the program:

```
0 is smaller than 100.0
5.88235 is smaller than 100.0
11.7647 is smaller than 100.0
17.6471 is smaller than 100.0
23.5294 is smaller than 100.0
29.4118 is smaller than 100.0
35.2941 is smaller than 100.0
41.1765 is smaller than 100.0
47.0588 is smaller than 100.0
52.9412 is smaller than 100.0
58.8235 is smaller than 100.0
64.7059 is smaller than 100.0
70.5882 is smaller than 100.0
76.4706 is smaller than 100.0
82.3529 is smaller than 100.0
88.2353 is smaller than 100.0
94.1176 is smaller than 100.0
100 is smaller than 100.0
105.882 is greater than 100.0
```

Notice how it differs from your expectations? Second to the last line says that 100 is smaller than 100.0, but how is that possible? We divide 100 by 17 and increment that amount 17 times, starting at 0. So we should end up with exactly 100 and the last line should read, "100 is equal to 100.0." Now try running the program again with the variable shape changed to 16, then you should get exactly what you expect to get. So how do we account for the fact that when 100 is split up to 17 portions evenly and we add them together, we do not get exactly 100? As a matter of fact, machines have their ways of handling floating-point numbers. For more information, please visit http://www.mathworks.com/moler/. The first chapter contains extensive information on how machines handle floating-point numbers, starting at page 34. By examining this example, you should learn that some bugs do not come from erroneous logic or syntax of the language but come from lack of understanding of how a compiler and an operating system work. Understanding these may take a long time, but you still can avoid the above situation by trial and error. If you do see a problem, try a couple of alternatives and see if you can figure out the source of the problem. Only by gaining more experience do your skills improve.

14.5 Case 5—cin

What does the following program do? Describe its behavior in plain English.

```
#include <iostream>
using namespace std;

int main(){
      char c;
      int counter = 0;
      cout << "Enter anything up until you enter a newline: ";
      cin >> c;
      while(c!='\n') {
          counter++;
          cin >> c;
      }
      cout << "You entered " << counter << " characters.\n";
      return 0;
}
```

Solution: At first it appears to count the number of characters the user has entered until a newline is entered, but this is not correct. If you run the program, you will realize that the program never terminates! Remember, **cin** ignores white spaces, which include spaces, tabs, and newlines. Therefore, **c** can never be a newline and the **while** loop never terminates. From this exercise you should learn that knowing only the superficial behavior of a C++ function never suffices; you need to go deeper and explore any exceptions associated with it. In this case, you know that **cin** receives inputs from the user, but you may not know that there are exceptions to that behavior: *It ignores white spaces.*

Whenever you use a function provided by C++ standard library, make sure you know what *exactly* it does, either by experimenting or looking it up online.

14.6   Case 6—prime number

The following program tests to see if an integer inputted by the user is a prime number. However, there are several bugs in it. Locate the bugs and correct them.

```
#include <iostream>
using namespace std;

bool isPrime(int n){
    if(n%2==0) return false;
    int m=3;
    while(m*m<n){
        if(n%m==0) return false;
        m += 2;
    }
    return true;
}
int main(){
    int input;
    cout<<"Please enter an integer: ";
    cin>>input;
    if(isPrime(input))
        cout<<input<<" is a prime number.\n";
    else
        cout<<input<<" is not a prime number.\n";
    return 0;
}
```

Solution: First of all, we need to know exactly what a prime number is. By definition, a prime number is an integer which is not evenly divisible by any integer except 1 and itself, with the exception that 1 is not a prime number. Therefore, the first several prime numbers are 2, 3, 5, 7, 11, 13. This concept should make it obvious that the first bug in this program is that it thinks 1 is a prime number. Also, **isPrime**() thinks that none of the even numbers is a prime number, but 2 is one.

Finally, we would like to know what the program thinks about perfect squares such as 9, 14, and 25. The **while** loop in **isPrime**() tests whether **m*m<n** because if **n** has any divisors other than 1 and itself, at least one of them must be less than Ön. For example, 9 is a prime; however, the **while** loop fails when **m** equals 3 (thus returns true). This should not happen, so we should change < to <=.

Here is the corrected program:

```
#include <iostream>
using namespace std;

bool isPrime(int n){
    if(n==2) return true;
    if(n%2==0 || n==1) return false;
    int m=3;
    while(m*m<=n){
        if(n%m==0) return false;
        m += 2;
    }
    return true;
}
int main(){
    int input;
    cout<<"Please enter an integer: ";
    cin>>input;
    if(isPrime(input))
        cout<<input<<" is a prime number.\n";
    else
        cout<<input<<" is not a prime number.\n";
    return 0;
}
```

By examining this exercise, you should have learned that a correctly working function is crucial for the correctness of a program. In this example there is only one function. What if you want to do more to the prime number the user enters?

You write more functions to process the number, and you end up getting incorrect results but are at a loss to figure out where they originate. Therefore, testing a function individually helps programmers locate a bug, if any. Also, correct logic is crucial to writing a good function. In this case, if we knew exactly what numbers are prime, we probably would not make any mistakes.

14.7 Case 7—factorial

This program is supposed to accept an integer and output its factorial, but it contains several bugs. Track them down and fix them.

```cpp
#include <iostream>
using namespace std;

int factorial(int n){
      int p=1;
      int i=n;
/* compute p = n * (n-1) * (n-2) * ... * 2 */
      while(i>=2);
      {
           i--;
           p=*i;
      }
      return i;
}
int main(){
      int input;
      cout<<"Please enter an integer: ";
      cin>>input;
      cout<<factorial(input)<<endl;
      return 0;
}
```

Solution: First of all, this program will not even compile. A programmer with keen eyes would spot the error right away; in the **while** loop p=*i should be p*=i. This is a simple syntax error. The second error is the semicolon after the **while** loop. The third error is i--; should be after p*=i, not before it. Sometimes in writing a loop you are little confused about whether the index should be incremented first or after some other code. By carefully going through the loop, you should be able to figure out the order in a jiffy. The last error is that **p** should be returned instead of **i**. What a function returns is also a common source of error. The variable **p** is what we want to return, not **i**. The following is the complete corrected program.

```cpp
#include <iostream>
using namespace std;

int factorial(int n){
    int p=1;
    int i=n;
/* compute p = n * (n-1) * (n-2) * ... * 2 */
    while(i>=2)
    {
        p*=i;
        i--;
    }
    return p;
}
int main(){
    int input;
    cout<<"Please enter an integer: ";
    cin>>input;
    cout<<factorial(input)<<endl;
    return 0;
}
```

14.8 Case 8—divide

The following program is supposed to receive two integers from the user and output the result of dividing the first one by the second one. However, it does not work properly. Point out where things go wrong.

```cpp
#include<iostream>
using namespace std;

int divide(int dividend, int divisor) {
    int result;
    result = dividend / divisor;
```

```
        return result;
}
int main(){
        int a, b, c;
        cout<<"Enter first integer: ";
        cin>>a;
        cout<<"Enter second integer: ";
        cin>>b;
        c = divide(a, b);
        cout<<a<<" divided by "<<b<<" is "<<c<<endl;
        return 0;
}
```

Solution: You should be able to point out that the result of the division is always an **int**, which means that it is inaccurate if it is supposed to be a floating-point number. Another bug is that when user enters 0 as the second integer, the program yields a segmentation fault. This is a small program and most of you probably see this bug already, but it demonstrates an important point I mentioned earlier—*preconditions of a function must be preserved*. In **divide**(), a precondition should be that the divisor must not be 0. However, we have no control over the user's inputs, so in order to preserve this precondition, we need to make sure that the divisor is not 0 before we do the division. One way is to use an **if** statement to see if the divisor is 0; if so, simply output an error message and terminate the program. Another way is to use **try** and **catch** blocks to handle that exception. Whatever you do, see to it that preconditions of a function are always preserved.

> Diamonds are merely carbon in its most concentrated form.

CHAPTER 15

Programming Exercises

"What? You didn't even lose a pound! What happened, Frank? I thought you already know you need to exercise to keep you fit," says Doctor Amy.

"Well, yes I do doc, I know everything you told me last time but still, I haven't lost a pound"

"Let's see here. Crunches?"

"Yes."

"Push-ups?"

"Checked."

"Sit-ups?"

"You got it."

"Man...looks like you've got everything here. How many times a day do you do crunches?"

"uh...zero.."

"What? You didn't do any of the exercises?"

"What are you talking about? You didn't say I needed to do them. You just told me I needed to know this, this, and that to stay fit..."

"@#$%^&"

So you see, no matter how much you think you know, without doing any exercises, you can't lose weight. For the sake of losing weight, get out your paper and start doing the following exercises, will ya?

15.1 Exercise #1: Groups of People

I remember in my freshman year I went to a concert in a concert hall, which was big enough to accommodate an audience of more than one thousand people. However only one or two hundred people showed up. As you can imagine "groups" began to form among those who knew each other or clicked in a casual conversation. Each group has some number of people sitting close to one another. Of course there were people who sat alone, myself included. Anyway, this piece of memory motivated this exercise. In this exercise consider a square board on which each square is either empty or occupied by one person. Two people belong to the same group if they share a common edge on the board. In Figure 15.1, there are 11 groups; the largest group has 5 people. Write a program that lists all groups. Specifically, the program reads a file, given by the command line, which contains the size of the board and the peoples' coordinates. The file that produces Figure 15.1 looks like this:

```
10 10
6 4
5 9
9 4
4 8
9 3
9 6
5 3
5 1
0 0
9 5
6 0
1 8
1 7
3 5
7 2
4 5
5 8
5 4
3 4
7 1
5 7
9 2
1 4
1 1
```

Of the very first pair, the first value is the width of the board and the second one the height of the board. In the following pairs, the first value is the horizontal coordinate and the second one the vertical coordinate. The lower left corner has coordinate (0,0); the vertical coordinate value increases upward and horizontal coordinate value increases eastward. The program determines which person belongs to which group, and outputs to a file the total number of groups, (for each group) the number of people the group has, and the coordinates of people

belonging to that group. Here is a sample output when the board looks likes
Figure 15.1:

There are a total of 11 group(s).

Group 1: 1 person(s).
  0 0

Group 2: 1 person(s).
  1 1

Group 3: 1 person(s).
  1 4

Group 4: 2 person(s).
  1 7
  1 8

Group 5: 3 person(s).
  3 4
  3 5
  4 5

Group 6: 4 person(s).
  4 8
  5 8
  5 9
  5 7

Group 7: 1 person(s).
  5 1

Group 8: 3 person(s).
  5 3
  5 4
  6 4

Group 9: 1 person(s).
  6 0

Group 10: 2 person(s).
    7 1
    7 2

Group 11: 5 person(s).
    9 2
    9 3
    9 4
    9 5
    9 6

Figure 15.1—a sample board with people (represented by circles)

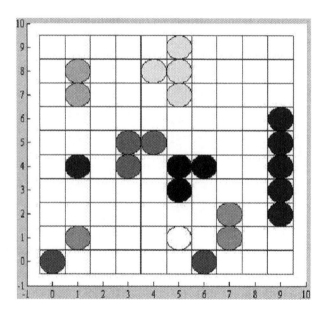

Suppose the program's executable is **group**, then the command line is

./group <inputFile> <outputFile>

Given all this information, you should be able to write the program now. Get started now and see if you are up to the challenge. If you are lost, take reference to my results, which follow our favorite four-step model.

Step 1: Let's think about the overall design of the program. First we declare a **bool** array of size specified by the user and initialize each element to false, indicating that no spots are occupied. Then we read in the locations of the people, making the corresponding elements in the array true. Now here comes the heart of the program: find all groups. One way to do it is to use recursion. For each occupied square, examine its surrounding squares recursively. After determining and listing all groups, we are done. As you can see, we do not really need to use a class; the recursive function can be written as a nonmember function. Here is my skeleton:

```
void process(int, int);

int main(int argc, char **argv){
- if arguments are not correct, give an error message and quit
- receive locations of people in the given file and assign proper values to all
squares on the grid
- go through each square on the grid, find the groups, and store them into a vector
- output results to the output file, specified by the command line
}


/*
precondition: x and y can never go out of the grid's bounds
postcondition: tempvx and tempvy will contain people belonging to a group
*/
void process(int x, int y) {
- mark square (x, y) handled
- store them in two vectors, tempvx and tempvy
- if the east square is occupied and not handled yet, call process on that square
- if the west square is occupied and not handled yet, call process on that square
- if the north square is occupied and not handled yet, call process on that square
- if the south square is occupied and not handled yet, call process on that square
}
```

You can, of course, find the groups without using a recursion. For example, scan the board and if a particular square is occupied, see if it belongs to any of the groups stored previously. If so, store it as belonging to that group. If not, store it as a new group. This algorithm works but it is not as cool as the recursive version, is it?

Step 2: Now let's figure out what variables we need. First we need two-dimensional arrays of **bool** to keep track of what square are occupied and which ones are handled. We need to know which squares are handled in the process of finding groups so that we do not examine the same square twice. We also need integers to store the width and height. We need file input and output objects to read from a file and write to a file. Finally, we need to store the groups somewhere, and this is a perfect time to use a **vector** because we don't know the number of groups ahead of time. We need **vectors** to keep track of locations of the people in a group, and we need **vectors** to store the groups we have found. Here is the refined skeleton:

```
void process(int, int);

int main(int argc, char **argv){
- if arguments are not correct, give an error message and quit

bool **occupy, **handled;
int width, height;
vector<int> tempvx, tempvy;
char *fileIn, *fileOut;
ifstream fin;
ofstream fout;
vector<vector<int> > groupX, groupY;

- receive locations of people in the given file and assign proper values to all
squares on the grid
- go through each square on the grid, find the groups, and store them into a
vector
- output results to the output file, specified by the command line
}

/*
precondition: x and y can never go out of the grid's bounds
postcondition: tempvx and tempvy will contain people belonging to a group
*/
void process(int x, int y) {
- same
}
```

Alternatively, I could've used a **vector** of a structure that holds 2 **int** instead of declared 2 **vector**, one for x coordinates and the other for y coordinates. Both are fine. Note that we may want some of the variables to have global scope so that we won't need to pass arguments from function calls to functions. This analysis will be done in the next step.

Step 3:
Interrelation: **tempvx, tempvy, groupX,** and **groupY** are **vector** and if you use [] to access their elements, be sure the index doesn't go out of their bounds.
State: **occupy** and **handled**, once changed, are changed for the lifetime of the program. **width** and **height** should never be changed once given by the file. **tempvx** and **tempvy** should be emptied after a group is determined so that they can be reused to get the next group. **groupX** and **groupY** keep on storing the groups until all groups are found.
Scope: Let's scrutinize **process()** and see what variables it needs access to. It needs **handled, occupied, tempvx, tempvy, width,** and **height.** It needs **width** and **height** to make sure the surrounding squares do not go out of the grid. We can make those 6 variables global. If doing so gives us too much trouble later, we can always change their scopes. The other variables can stay local.

Given this information, let's update our skeleton:

```
bool **occupy, **handled;
int width, height;
vector<int> tempvx, tempvy;

void process(int, int);
int main(int argc, char **argv){
- if arguments are not correct, give an error message and quit
     char *fileIn, *fileOut;
     ifstream fin;
     ofstream fout;
     vector<vector<int> > groupX, groupY;
- receive locations of people in the given file and assign proper values to all
squares on the grid
- go through each square on the grid, find the groups, and store them into a
vector
- output results to the output file, specified by the command line
}

/*
precondition: x and y can never go out of the grid's bounds
postcondition: tempvx and tempvy will contain people belonging to a group
```

```
*/
void process(int x, int y) {
- same
}
```

Keep in mind that we may need more variables as we code.

Step 4: The program is rather straightforward and easy to code. The following is the complete program.

```
/*
Michael Wen
6/6/2003
Given the size of the grid and the layout of people, this program outputs rele-
vant information about each group on the grid.
*/
#include<iostream>
#include<fstream>
#include<vector>
using namespace std;

int width, height, total;
vector<int> tempvx, tempvy;
bool **occupy, **handled;

void process(int, int);

int main(int argc, char **argv){
/* if arguments are not correct, give an error message and quit */
    if(argc!=3){
        cout<<"usage: ./exe <inputFile> <outputFile>\n";
        cout<<"<inputFile>: input file's name\n";
        cout<<"<outputFile>: output file's name\n";
        exit(1);
    }
    int i,j;
    char *fileIn, *fileOut;
    ifstream fin;
    ofstream fout;
    vector<vector<int> > groupX, groupY;
```

/* receive locations of people in the given file and assign proper values to all squares on the grid */

```
fileIn=argv[1];
fileOut=argv[2];
fin.open(fileIn);
fin>>width;
fin>>height;
occupy = new bool*[width];
handled = new bool*[width];
for(i=0;i<width;i++){
        occupy[i] = new bool[height];
        handled[i] = new bool[height];
}
for(i=0;i<width;i++)
        for(j=0;j<height;j++)
                handled[i][j]=occupy[i][j]=false;
while(fin) {
        fin>>i;
        fin>>j;
        if(i<0 || i>=width || j<0 || j>=height)
                continue;
        occupy[i][j]=true;
}
fin.close();
```

/* go through each square on the grid, find the groups, and store them into a vector */

```
for(i=0;i<width;i++)
        for(j=0;j<height;j++)
                if(occupy[i][j] && !handled[i][j]){
                        process(i,j);
                        groupX.push_back(tempvx);
                        groupY.push_back(tempvy);
                        tempvx.clear();
                        tempvy.clear();
                }
total=groupX.size();
```

/* output results to the output file, specified by the command line */

```
        fout.open(fileOut);
        fout<<"There are a total of "<<total<<" group(s).\n\n";
        for(i=0;i<total;i++){
            tempvx=groupX[i];
            tempvy=groupY[i];
            fout<<"Group "<<i+1<<": "<<tempvx.size()<<" person(s).\n";
            for(j=0;j<tempvx.size();j++)
                fout<<"\t"<<tempvx[j]<<' '<<tempvy[j]<<endl;
            fout<<endl;
        }
        fout.close();
        return 0;
}


/*
precondition: x and y can never go out of the board's bounds
postcondition: tempvx and tempvy will contain people belonging to a group
*/
void process(int x, int y) {
/* mark square (x, y) handled */
        handled[x][y]=true;
/* store it in a vector */
        tempvx.push_back(x);
        tempvy.push_back(y);
/* if the east square is occupied and not handled, call process on that square */
        if(x<width-1 && occupy[x+1][y] && !handled[x+1][y])
            process(x+1,y);
/* if the west square is occupied and not handled, call process on that square */
        if(x>0 && occupy[x-1][y] && !handled[x-1][y])
            process(x-1,y);
/* if the north square is occupied and not handled, call process on that square */
        if(y<height-1 && occupy[x][y+1] && !handled[x][y+1])
            process(x,y+1);
/* if the south square is occupied and not handled, call process on that square */
        if(y>0 && occupy[x][y-1] && !handled[x][y-1])
            process(x,y-1);
}
```

This program does minimal error-checking, and you can enhance it so that no matter what the input file looks like, your program will handle it properly. You can also write a program to generate random input files to test your program. Inside **process**() we see that the **if** statements take advantage of the short-circuit evaluation, which is discussed in <u>Section 16.5</u>. Note that array-out-of-bounds errors are easy to make in this program, so be careful.

15.2   Exercise #2: The Game of Nim

There are many variations of the game of Nim. In this program you are to allow the user to play this game with the computer. The game starts with an initial number of marbles, which your program decides, and determines at random who goes first, and then the user and the computer take turns. The player who goes gets a chance to draw a certain number of marbles which must be at least one and no greater than half of the current number of marbles. For example, if there are 15 marbles currently, the player can draw up to 7 marbles. The player who draws the last marbles loses the game. To make the program even more interesting and challenging, you will need to devise a stupid approach as well as a smart approach for the computer player. The approach the computer plays is determined at the start of the game at random. In the stupid approach, the computer simply draws a random legal number of marbles. In the smart approach, the computer needs to do the following things:

- If the current number of marbles is equal to a power of 2 minus 1, then the computer simply draws a random legal number of marbles.
- Otherwise, the computer takes a number of marbles so that the number of the remaining marbles is equal to a power of 2 minus 1.

If you want to know the logic behind it, do a little experiment and see for yourself. A smart computer should always win unless the first situation occurs (the current number of marbles is equal to a power of 2 minus 1). For example, if the current number of marbles is 78, the smart computer should take 15 marbles away, leaving 63 marbles, which is $2^6 - 1$. The behavior of the program can be seen from the following sample runs. Here is a sample run when the computer plays dumb:

****** Welcome to the game of Nim ******
The number of marbles you draw must be > 0 and <= half of the total marbles.
The person who gets the last marble loses.

You go first.
Initial number of marbles: 15

The computer is playing stupid.
Enter number of marble(s) to draw: 6
Current number of marble(s): 9

Computer takes off 2 marble(s).
Current number of marble(s): 7

Enter number of marble(s) to draw: 3
Current number of marble(s): 4

Computer takes off 2 marble(s).
Current number of marble(s): 2

Enter number of marble(s) to draw: 2
Enter number of marble(s) to draw: 1
Current number of marble(s): 1

You win!

Here is a sample run when the computer plays smart:

****** Welcome to the game of Nim ******
The number of marbles you draw must be > 0 and <= half of the total marbles.
The person who gets the last marble loses.

You go first.
Initial number of marbles: 98
The computer is playing smart.
Enter number of marble(s) to draw: 1
Current number of marble(s): 97

Computer takes off 34 marble(s).
Current number of marble(s): 63

Enter number of marble(s) to draw: 2
Current number of marble(s): 61

Computer takes off 30 marble(s).
Current number of marble(s): 31

Enter number of marble(s) to draw: 3
Current number of marble(s): 28

Computer takes off 13 marble(s).
Current number of marble(s): 15

Enter number of marble(s) to draw: 4
Current number of marble(s): 11

Computer takes off 4 marble(s).
Current number of marble(s): 7

Enter number of marble(s) to draw: 3
Current number of marble(s): 4

Computer takes off 1 marble(s).
Current number of marble(s): 3

Enter number of marble(s) to draw: 2
Enter number of marble(s) to draw: 1
Current number of marble(s): 2

Computer takes off 1 marble(s).
Current number of marble(s): 1

The computer wins!

The format of the output is not important, but make sure you include the key elements. Now that you have enough information, get started on this program. As usual, take reference to my results only when you've racked your brain and still cannot finish the program.

Step 1: The program flow should be straightforward. The catch lies in how the computer in smart mode makes its move. We need a function to determine whether the current number of marbles is one less than a power of 2. We also need a function to calculate the number of marbles the smart computer should draw. The following is my skeleton:

```
bool deadNum(int);
int compute(int);
```

```
int main() {
- initialize random number generator
- introduce the game of Nim and display its rules
- determine who goes first and the initial number of marbles
- deal with the case when computer plays stupid
        if it's user's turn, prompt user to enter a number
                if the number is invalid, prompt user to enter another one
        if it's computer's turn, draw a random legal number of marbles
- deal with the case when computer plays smart
        if it's user's turn, prompt user to enter a number
                if the number is invalid, prompt user to enter another one
        if it's computer's turn, draw a number of marbles based on the strategy
- switch turn
}


/*
precondition: n must be a positive integer
postcondition: return true if n is 1 less than any power of 2; return false otherwise
*/
bool deadNum(int n) {
- return true if n is a power of 2 minus 1
}


/*
precondition: n must be a positive integer
postcondition: return the number of marbles smart computer should draw
*/
int compute(int n) {
- calculate the largest possible number which is 1 less than a power of 2
- return (n – that number)
}
```

Step 2: Now let's determine what variables we need. We need 7 **int** to store the highest possible number of marbles initially, the lowest possible number of marbles initially, the current number of marbles, the current turn, the number of marbles computer draws at a particular turn, the number of marbles the user draws at a particular turn, and the mode the computer adopts. By the way, there is something wrong with the skeleton; the game should be played until one side loses, so we need a loop. Here is my refined skeleton:

```
bool deadNum(int);
int compute(int);

int main() {
        int max, min, size, whoseTurn, compTakeOff, youTakeOff, mode;
```

- initialize random number generator
- introduce the game of Nim and display its rules
- determine who goes first and the initial number of marbles
- deal with the case when computer plays stupid
        while the number of marbles is >= 1
                if it's user's turn, prompt user to enter a number
                        if the number is invalid, prompt user to enter another one
                if it's computer's turn, draw a random legal number of marbles
                switch turn
- deal with the case when computer plays smart
        while the number of marbles is >= 1
                if it's user's turn, prompt user to enter a number
                        if the number is invalid, prompt user to enter another one
                if it's computer's turn, draw a number of marbles based on the strategy
                switch turn

```
}
```

```
/*
precondition: n must be a positive integer
postcondition: return true if n is 1 less than any power of 2; return false otherwise
*/
bool deadNum(int n) {
- same
}
```

```
/*
precondition: n must be a positive integer
postcondition: return the number of marbles smart computer should draw
*/
int compute(int n) {
- same
}
```

Step 3:
Interrelation: All variables are independent of one another.
State: **max** and **min** are determined by the programmer and shouldn't change throughout the program; **size** is the current number of marbles and is always decreasing; **whoseTurn** should switch back and forth between player and computer; **compTakeOff** and **youTakeOff** should be legal number of marbles to draw; **mode** should not change once it is determined.
Scope: Out of these variables, we can make **max** and **min** global constants because their values do not change throughout the program.

Here's the updated skeleton:

```
bool deadNum(int);
int compute(int);
const int MAX = 91;
const int MIN = 13;

int main() {
     int size, whoseTurn, compTakeOff, youTakeOff, mode;
- same
}

/*
precondition: n should be a positive integer
postcondition: return true if n is 1 less than any power of 2; return false other-
wise
*/
bool deadNum(int n) {
- same
}

/*
precondition: n should be a positive integer
postcondition: return the number of marbles smart computer should draw
*/
int compute(int n) {
- same
}
```

Step 4: Here is a complete program following the above skeleton:

```
/*
Michael Wen
6/5/2003
This program plays a game of Nim with the user.
*/
#include <iostream>
#include <cmath>
#include <ctime>
using namespace std;

bool deadNum(int);
int compute(int);
const int MAX = 91;
const int MIN = 13;

int main() {
    int size, whoseTurn, compTakeOff, youTakeOff, mode;

/* initialize random number generator */
    srand(time(0));
/* introduce the game of Nim and display its rules */
    cout << "\n****** Welcome to the game of Nim ******\n";
    cout << "The number of marbles you draw must be > 0 and <= half of the
        total marbles.\n";
    cout << "The person who gets the last marble loses.\n\n";

/* determine who goes first and the initial number of marbles */
    whoseTurn = rand() % 2;
    if(whoseTurn==0)
        cout << "Computer goes first.\n";
    else
        cout << "You go first.\n";
    size = MIN + rand() % (MAX-MIN);
    cout << "Initial number of marbles: " << size << endl;
    mode = rand() % 2;

/* deal with the case when computer plays stupid */
    if (mode==0) {
```

```
                    cout << "The computer is playing stupid.\n";

                    while (size!=1) {
                        if (whoseTurn==0) {
/* draw a random legal number of marbles */
                            compTakeOff = 1 + rand() % (size / 2);
                            size -= compTakeOff;
                            cout << "Computer takes off " << compTakeOff <<
                            " marble(s).\n";
                            cout << "Current number of marble(s): " << size << "\n\n";
                        }
                        else {
/* prompt user to enter a number */
                            do {
                                cout << "Enter number of marble(s) to draw: ";
                                cin >> youTakeOff;
                            } while(youTakeOff<=0 || youTakeOff>size/2);
                            size -= youTakeOff;
                            cout << "Current number of marble(s): " << size << "\n\n";
                        }
                        whoseTurn = whoseTurn==0 ? 1 : 0;
                    }
                }
/* deal with the case when computer plays smart */
            else {
                    cout << "The computer is playing smart.\n";
                    while (size!=1) {
                        if (whoseTurn==0) {
                            if (deadNum(size)) {
/* draw a random legal number of marbles */
                                compTakeOff = 1 + rand() % (size / 2);
                                size -= compTakeOff;
                                cout << "Computer takes off " << compTakeOff;
                                cout << " marble(s).\n";
                                cout << "Current number of marble(s): " << size
                                << "\n\n";
                            }
                            else {
/* use the strategy */
                                compTakeOff = compute(size);
```

```
                        size -= compTakeOff;
                        cout << "Computer takes off " << compTakeOff;
                        cout << " marble(s).\n";
                        cout << "Current number of marble(s): " << size
                    << "\n\n";
                        }
                }
                else {
                    do {
                        cout << "Enter number of marble(s) to draw: ";
                        cin >> youTakeOff;
                    } while (youTakeOff <= 0 || youTakeOff > size / 2);
                    size -= youTakeOff;
                    cout << "Current number of marble(s): " << size << "\n\n";
                    }
                whoseTurn = whoseTurn==0 ? 1 : 0;
            }
        }
        if (whoseTurn == 1)
            cout << "The computer wins!" << endl;
        else
            cout << "You win!" << endl;
        return 0;
}

/*
precondition: n should be a positive integer
postcondition: return true if n is 1 less than any power of 2; return false otherwise
*/
bool deadNum(int n) {
    int i = -1;
    while((int)pow(2.0,++i) < n)
            ;
    return ((int)pow(2.0, i)==n+1);
}

/*
precondition: n should be a positive integer
postcondition: return the number of marbles smart computer should draw
*/
```

```
int compute(int n) {
    int i = -1;
    while((int)pow(2.0,++i) < n)
            ;
    i--;
    return n - ((int)pow(2.0, i) - 1);
}
```

After we run it a couple of times, it seems to work perfectly when computer is playing stupid. It, however, does not work property when computer is playing smart. When the current number of marbles is down to 2 and it's computer's turn, it takes away 2 marbles. You can insert several print statements before each function call and you will find that **compute()** is responsible for this bug. If **n** is 2, **i** turns out to be 1, and **i–** gives 0. So the function returns 2, and computer draws 2 marbles. This function does not work when **n** equals 2. Let's fix it by simply handling it as an exception. Here is the new version of **compute()**:

```
/*
preconditions: n should be a positive integer
postconditions: returns the number of marbles smart computer should draw
exceptions: when n is 2, return 1
*/
int compute(int n) {
    if(n==2)
            return 1;
    int i = -1;
    while((int)pow(2.0,++i) < n)
            ;
    i--;
    return n - ((int)pow(2.0, i) - 1);
}
```

Now everything works perfectly; however, this program contains redundant code, so it's possible to reduce its code size. Your program could be shorter and cleaner than mine. Note that the program does not do any error checking. If you enter a letter when a number is expected, the program runs into a loop. You can fix it by using <stdlib.h>'s **atoi()** to convert a **char** array to an **int**. If **atoi()** returns 0, then either an error has occurred or the user enters 0. You will have plenty of opportunities to sharpen your error-checking skills in the coming programming exercises.

15.3 Exercise #3: The Eight Queens' Puzzle

Some of you probably have heard of this famous puzzle. You have an 8-by-8 square board and you have 8 queens. You place them on the board so that none of the queens is able to conflict with another queen. In chess, a queen can move horizontally, vertically, and diagonally for however many units. So basically you make sure they cannot attack each other. Now that you have enough information, go ahead and write a program to solve this puzzle. You need to find all solutions possible, not just one. Here are the suggested specifications for the program:

- User runs the program with no argument in command line.
- The program outputs all the solutions onto screen like the following (X is a queen):

```
Solution: 1
*01234567*
0X        0
1     X   1
2         X2
3      X  3
4  X      4
5        X 5
6 X       6
7    X    7
*01234567*

Solution: 2
*01234567*
0X        0
1     X   1
2         X2
3  X      3
4        X 4
5   X     5
6 X       6
7     X   7
*01234567*
.
.
.
```

.

```
Solution:  12
*01234567*
0  X        0
1      X    1
2 X         2
3      X    3
4          X4
5X          5
6         X 6
7   X       7
*01234567*
```

In fact, I'd like the program to be flexible. Your program needs to be able to deal with square boards of every size, not just 8-by-8. You specify it in your program and compile and run it to get the corresponding results. For example if you specify the board size to be 10-by-10, that means there are ten queens waiting to be placed on the board, and your program finds solutions to it. You can make it so that user decides the board size in command line, but that is a trivial modification. Ready to roll? Let's play the eight queens' puzzle.

Step 1: The idea is to use recursion to find a board configuration where no two queens can attack each other. We put one queen somewhere, check if the board is okay; if it is okay put the next queen; if it is not okay we put the queen somewhere else. We go on until we reach a solution, in which case we check whether it is repeated or not. We output it if it is not repeated. We try to find the next solution until we try every possible configuration of the board. Here is my pseudocode of the program:

```
void recur(int cur);
bool repeated();
bool conflict();

int main(int argc, char **argv) {
- run the recursive function given the size of the board
}

/*
precondition: cur and ii should both contain positive values
```

postcondition: recursively find a board configuration where no two queens can attack each other
*/
void recur(int cur){
- if cur is 0 it is the base case
     if current solution is not repeated
         put it in a vector
         output it onto screen
         return
- else
     loop through each position on the board
         fill the position with a queen
         if no queens are in conflict with one another
             call recur(cur-1) to place the next queen
         else
             un-fill the position
}

/*
precondition: none
postcondition: return true if b is an orientation contained in va; b is not changed
*/
bool repeated(){
- return true if current board configuration is repeated, meaning that it has been outputted before already; note it needs to check every transposition and rotation to make sure it is not repeated; return false otherwise
}

/*
precondition: none
postcondition: return true if there is conflict among the queens on b; return false otherwise
*/
bool conflict(){
- return true if no queens are in conflict with one another; return false otherwise
}

The argument to **recur**() is the number of queens that are waiting to be placed on the board. So if it is zero, it means we successfully place every queen and can output the board configuration if it is not repeated. As you can see everything is straightforward, but when it gets down to implementing it we may need to move things around or add something to avoid a problem or to achieve a task. We will see.

Step 2: Obviously we need to represent the board somehow, and I'd use a wrapper structure to wrap a two-dimensional **int** array. You can use **bool** array or another data structure if you want to. I use 1 to represent an empty position and 0 to represent a position occupied by a queen. I need an integer to indicate the size of the board so that by simply changing it the program can find solutions to other numbers of queens. I need a vector to store past solutions so that I do not output the same solution twice. I need several variables to do indexing in loops, but they are not that important. While reviewing my previous skeleton I realize that in **recur()** when the board successfully places a queen it calls **recur()** recursively to place the next queen. However I do not want **recur()** to start from the beginning of the loop trying to place the queen because the previous positions are tried already and there is no point trying them again. So I think I need to give **recur()** one more argument to tell it where to begin in the loop so as to increase efficiency. Here is my updated skeleton:

```
const int MAX = 8;
struct array {
      Int arr[MAX], arr[MAX];
}
vector<array> va;
array board;  //board configuration

void recur(int cur);
bool repeated();
bool conflict();

int main(int argc, char **argv) {
- run the recursive function given the size of the board
}

/*
precondition: cur and ii should both contain positive values
postcondition: recursively find a board configuration where no two queens
can attack each other
*/
void recur(int cur, int ii){
```

- if cur is 0 it is the base case
>   if current solution is not repeated
>>   put it in a vector
>>   output it onto screen
>>   return
- else
>   loop through each position on the board starting from ii
>>   fill the position with a queen
>>   if no queens are in conflict with one another
>>>   call recur(cur-1, cur_pos) to place the next queen
>>   else
>>>   un-fill the position
}

```
/*
precondition: none
postcondition: return true if b is an orientation contained in va; b is not changed
*/
bool repeated(){
- same
}
```

```
/*
precondition: none
postcondition: return true if there is conflict among the queens on b; return false
otherwise
*/
bool conflict(){
- same
}
```

Step 3: Now everything should be clear and you should be able to take over from here if you haven't written the program yourself. Now we need to explore the program more deeply, making sure how variables are connected and so on.

Interrelation: There are several loops in the program and the index of each loop should not go out of bounds of the arrays that use it. In **recur**() pay special attention to the indices of the nested **for** loops because they may be used as parameter in **recur**(). Also pay attention to **conflict**() because you will need to perform vertical, horizontal, and diagonal testing on the board configuration to make sure no queens can attack another queen. In this case loops are used heavily and index-out-of-bound errors or logic errors are easy to make.

<u>State</u>: Once **MAX** is assigned a value it should not change through the program. The board configuration, **board**, will be used intensively in the program, so its values are changed constantly. If they are changed momentarily for testing purposes be sure to restore their previous values. **va** should start out with nothing in it and accrue more and more unique solutions until it stores every possible solution.

<u>Scope</u>: As discussed, value in **MAX** should not change once assigned, so it deserves a constant, global scope. **board** and **va** can be either global or local, and I'd like to make them global so that they do not need to be passed around from function to function.

Step 4: While implementing it I realize **board** is used very often, so I just rename it to **b** for brevity. To make sure no repeated solutions are reported, I need to write **transpose**(), to transpose a board so that every column is switched with every corresponding row, and **rotate90**(), to rotate a board 90 degrees counterclockwise, to find every possible equivalent board configuration of a given one. For example, the following two boards are considered equivalent, assuming the board size is 4:

```
*0123*
0X    0
1X    1
2X    2
3     3
*0123*

*0123*
0     0
1     1
2     2
3XXX3
*0123*
```

Since the second board is the first board after rotating 90 degrees counterclockwise. **transpose**() is a no-brainer but **rotate90**() takes some skills, so code **rotate90**() by yourself to prove you are made of something, will you?

Here is the complete program:

```
/*
Michael Wen
6/8/2003
This program solves the classic eight queens' puzzle.
*/
#include <iostream>
#include <vector>
using namespace std;

const int MAX = 8;
struct array {
      int arr[MAX][MAX];
};
int counter;
array b;
vector<array> va;

bool repeated();
void makeEqual(array&, array&);
bool operator==(array&, array&);
void transpose(array&);
void rotate90(array&);
void outputBoard();
void initArray(array&);
bool conflict();
void recur(int, int);

int main() {
      int cur;
      bool found;

      initArray(b);
      cur = MAX;
      found = false;
      counter = 1;
/* run the recursive function given the size of the board */
      recur(cur, -1);
      return 0;
```

```
}

/*
precondition: none
postcondition: return true if b is an orientation contained in va; b is not
changed
*/
bool repeated() {
    int i;
    array tempa;
    makeEqual(tempa, b);
/* rotate and transpose each element in va and test if b matches any of it */
    for(i=0; i<va.size(); i++) {
        if(tempa==va[i])
            return true;
    }
    makeEqual(tempa, b);
    rotate90(tempa);
    for(i=0; i<va.size(); i++) {
        if(tempa==va[i])
            return true;
    }
    makeEqual(tempa, b);
    rotate90(tempa);
    rotate90(tempa);
    for(i=0; i<va.size(); i++) {
        if(tempa==va[i])
            return true;
    }
    makeEqual(tempa, b);
    rotate90(tempa);
    rotate90(tempa);
    rotate90(tempa);
    for(i=0; i<va.size(); i++) {
        if(tempa==va[i])
            return true;
    }
    makeEqual(tempa, b);
    transpose(tempa);
    for(i=0; i<va.size(); i++) {
```

```
                if(tempa==va[i])
                    return true;
        }
        makeEqual(tempa, b);
        transpose(tempa);
        rotate90(tempa);
        for(i=0; i<va.size(); i++) {
            if(tempa==va[i])
                    return true;
        }
        makeEqual(tempa, b);
        transpose(tempa);
        rotate90(tempa);
        rotate90(tempa);
        for(i=0; i<va.size(); i++) {
            if(tempa==va[i])
                    return true;
        }
        makeEqual(tempa, b);
        transpose(tempa);
        rotate90(tempa);
        rotate90(tempa);
        rotate90(tempa);
        for(i=0; i<va.size(); i++) {
            if(tempa==va[i])
                    return true;
        }
        return false;
}

/*
precondition: none
postcondition: equate b with a
*/
void makeEqual(array & a, array & b) {
        int i, i2;
        for(i=0; i<MAX; ++i)
            for(i2=0; i2<MAX; ++i2)
                a.arr[i][i2] = b.arr[i][i2];
}
```

```
/*
precondition: none
postcondition: return true if a contains identical elements as b
*/
bool operator==(array & a, array & b) {
    int i, i2;
    for(i=0; i<MAX; ++i)
        for(i2=0; i2<MAX; ++i2)
            if(a.arr[i][i2]!=b.arr[i][i2])
                return false;
    return true;
}

/*
precondition: none
postcondition: transpose a
*/
void transpose(array & a) {
    array tempa;
    int r, c;

    initArray(tempa);
    for(r=0; r<MAX; r++)
        for(c=0; c<MAX; c++)
            tempa.arr[r][c] = a.arr[c][r];
    makeEqual(a, tempa);
}

/*
precondition: none
postcondition: rotate a by 90 degrees counterclockwise
*/
void rotate90(array & a) {
    int r, c;
    bool found = false;
    array tempa;

    initArray(tempa);
    for(r=0; r<MAX; r++)
```

```
        for(c=0; c<MAX; c++)
            if(MAX-c-1>=0)
                tempa.arr[MAX-c-1][r] = a.arr[r][c];
    makeEqual(a, tempa);
}
```

```
/*
precondition: none
postcondition: output the board configuration represented by b
*/
void outputBoard() {
    int i, i2;
    cout << "*";
    for(i=0; i<MAX; i++)
        cout << i;
    cout << "*\n";
    for(i=0; i<MAX; i++) {
        cout << i;
        for(i2=0; i2<MAX; i2++)
            if(b.arr[i][i2]==0)
                cout << 'X';
            else
                cout << ' ';
        cout << i << endl;
    }
    cout << "*";
    for(i=0; i<MAX; i++)
        cout << i;
    cout << "*\n";
}
```

```
/*
precondition: none
postcondition: each element in a is initialized to 1, meaning empty
*/
void initArray(array & a) {
    int i, i2;
    for(i=0; i<MAX; i++)
        for(i2=0; i2<MAX; i2++)
            a.arr[i][i2] = 1;
```

```
}

/*
precondition: none
postcondition: return true if there is conflict among the queens on b; return
false otherwise
*/
bool conflict() {
    int i, i2, j, j2;
    for(i=0; i<MAX; i++)
        for(i2=0; i2<MAX; i2++)
            if(b.arr[i][i2]==0) {
/* vertical and horizontal */
                for(j=0; j<MAX; j++) {
                    if(b.arr[j][i2]==0&&j!=i)
                        return true;
                    if(b.arr[i][j]==0&&j!=i2)
                        return true;
                }
/* upper left to lower right */
                j = i-1;
                j2 = i2-1;
                while(j>=0 && j2>=0) {
                    if(b.arr[j][j2]==0)
                        return true;
                    j--;
                    j2--;
                }
                j = i+1;
                j2 = i2+1;
                while(j<MAX && j2<MAX) {
                    if(b.arr[j][j2]==0)
                        return true;
                    j++;
                    j2++;
                }
/* upper right to lower left */
                j = i-1;
                j2 = i2+1;
                while(j>=0 && j2<MAX) {
```

```
                              if(b.arr[j][j2]==0)
                                      return true;
                              j--;
                              j2++;
                          }
                          j = i+1;
                          j2 = i2-1;
                          while(j<MAX && j2>=0) {
                                  if(b.arr[j][j2]==0)
                                          return true;
                                  j++;
                                  j2--;
                          }
                  }
          return false;
}


/*
precondition: cur and ii should both contain positive values
postcondition: recursively find a board configuration where no two queens
can attack each other
*/
void recur(int cur, int ii) {
/* if cur is 0 it is the base case */
      if(cur==0) {
/* if current solution is not repeated */
              if(!repeated()) {
/* put it in a vector */
                      va.push_back(b);
                      cout << "\nSolution: " << counter << endl;
                      ++counter;
/* output it onto screen */
                      outputBoard();
              }
              return;
      }
      int i, i2;
/* loop through each position on the board starting from ii */
      for(i=ii+1; i<MAX; i++) {
            for(i2=0; i2<MAX; i2++) {
```

```
              if(b.arr[i][i2]==1) {
/* fill the position with a queen */
                  b.arr[i][i2]=0;
/* if no queens are in conflict with one another */
                  if(!conflict())
/* call recur() to place the next queen */
                      recur(cur-1, i);
/* un-fill the position */
                  b.arr[i][i2]=1;
              }
          }
      }
}
```

Congratulations if you worked this out by yourself. You've certainly gained more experience with writing recursive functions. Care to move on?

15.4   Exercise #4: Word Ladder Game

Many of you probably have heard of this game. You give the size of the "ladder" and the computer generates two words, the beginning word and the destination word, for you. You must come up with another word which is exactly one letter different from the beginning word. Then you come up with another word which is exactly one letter different from the one you just came up with. This process goes on until you either reach the destination word or you run out of the chances. For example, if the ladder size is 3 and the beginning and destination words are "dank" and "bale", respectively, then you can come up with the following sequence:

dank – bank – balk – bale

Then you win the game. There are many subtle points in the implementation, however. For example, if the ladder size is 3 and the beginning and destination words are "dank" and "bank", respectively, then the following sequence

dank – bank – dank – bank

is a valid word ladder. If most word ladders the computer generates look like this one, the player would feel pretty upset. Therefore, let's make it a rule that no words in a ladder may be repeated. Also, to make life easier, let's assume that all words are 4-letter words. The following are the program's specifications:

- Start by reading a file, given in command line, that contains a list of valid 4-letter words. If not all words are 4-letter words, either output an error message and terminate the program or ignore invalid words and continue.
- Ask the user for the size of the word ladder, which must be between 1 and 20, inclusively.
- Search through all valid words and find such a word ladder
- If a word ladder cannot be found (probably the word list is too small or the ladder size too big), output an error message and terminate the program.
- Prompt the user to enter a word ladder, given the beginning and destination words.
- If the user enters an invalid word, prompt him or her to enter again.
- You may add extra functionality such as the ability to quit at any time, the ability to restart at any time, and the ability to show a sample solution.
- Under no circumstances should your program crash. Therefore, you must do proper error-checking to ensure that even the most wacky psychotic can't break it.

You can also make it menu-driven and allow the user to play the game many times, but they are trivial features. What you should get out of writing this program is how to do exhaustive error-checking. Here is one sample run:

```
./ladder words.txt
Enter a ladder size (1 to 20 inclusively): a
Enter a ladder size (1 to 20 inclusively): yes
Enter a ladder size (1 to 20 inclusively): 123
Enter a ladder size (1 to 20 inclusively): -123
Enter a ladder size (1 to 20 inclusively): 4
At any time, enter q to exit the game, r to restart the game,
and s to show solution.

Enter words from sect to heat:
sect
sept
seat
teat
heat
```

Congratulations!

Here's another sample run:

./ladder words.txt
Enter a ladder size (1 to 20 inclusively): 4
At any time, enter q to exit the game, r to restart the game,
and s to show solution.

Enter words from rove to love:
rove
love
lote
lote is not valid. Enter a new word: lave
lave is not valid. Enter a new word: 1234
1234 is not valid. Enter a new word: dadadalla
dadadalla is not valid. Enter a new word: dove
move
mole

I am sorry. Please try again next time.

You shouldn't expect the player to enter the identical ladder as the one your program finds. For example, from bake to sale with ladder size being 2, you can do

bake – sake – sale

or

bake – bale – sale

Both are fine, provided all words are in the input file. Now you should be able to write the program. This program is probably bigger and harder than any of the earlier ones you wrote, so get started immediately. There are many procrastinators out there, and I'm sure you are not one of them. Go go go!

As usual, I provide my own skeletons and code. You shouldn't refer to them unless you are stuck and desperate. Remember, *one day you will be totally on your own, so it's up to you whether you should sharpen yours skills now or suffer later.*

Step 1: Since a valid word is only 4-letter long, there are 26*26*26*26 possible combinations. Therefore, I use a 4-dimensional **bool** array to store valid words. I could store them into a string vector, but searching would take a long time. The heart of the program is **ladder()**, which takes a **string**, an **int**, and a **bool**. It basically finds and stores a solution into a **vector**. If this solution is not found, **success** is still false and we should pick a different beginning word next time. If no words can form a valid word ladder, we simply output an error message. Here is my skeleton:

```
bool isValid(string, string);
void ladder(string, int, bool&);
bool isRepeated(string);
void remove(string);
bool allLetter(string);

int main(int argc, char **argv) {
- exit if no file is provided in command line
- initialize the random number generator
- use a 4-dimensional bool array to store valid words
- prompt the user to enter a valid ladder size
- find a word ladder of that size
      if found, continue
      if not found, issue an error message and exit
- start the game by having the user input the intermediate words in the word
ladder, given the beginning and destination words
- output results depending on how the user did
}

/*
precondition: first and second must consist of only letters and must be of length 4
postcondition: return true if transition from first to second is valid and second
is a word in the word list
*/
bool isValid(string first, string second) {
- return true if second word is a valid word and is exactly one letter different
from first
- return false otherwise
}
```

```
/*
precondition: success should be false in the first function call
        t should be >= 1
        w must be a 4-letter string
postcondition: success is set true if the word ladder has been found
*/
void ladder(string w, int t, bool & success) {
- put w into the solution vector
- if t is 0, set success to true and return
- iterate from 'a' through 'z' in the first letter of w
        if the new word is a valid word and is not in the solution vector, that
        means this is a valid word in the ladder. So call ladder recursively with
        this new word.
- iterate from 'a' through 'z' in the second letter of w
        if the new word is a valid word and is not in the solution vector, that
        means this is a valid word in the ladder. So call ladder recursively with
        this new word.
- iterate from 'a' through 'z' in the third letter of w
        if the new word is a valid word and is not in the solution vector, that
        means this is a valid word in the ladder. So call ladder recursively with
        this new word.
- iterate from 'a' through 'z' in the fourth letter of w
        if the new word is a valid word and is not in the solution vector, that
        means this is a valid word in the ladder. So call ladder recursively with
        this new word.
}


/*
precondition: w can be any string
postcondition: return true if w is in the word list; return false otherwise
*/
bool isRepeated(string w) {
- return true if w is inside the word ladder vector; return false otherwise
}


/*
precondition: w can be any string
postcondition: remove w from the word list
*/
void remove(string w) {
```

- remove w from the word list vector so that we do not use it as the beginning word twice
}

```
/*
precondition: w must be a 4-character string
postcondition: return true if w is alphabetic; return false otherwise
*/
bool allLetter(string w) {
- return true if w consists of exactly 4 English letters
}
```

Step 2: As for variables, we need a 4-dimensional **bool** array to store valid 4-letter words, 4 **int** to initialize the array, a **string vector** to store a solution, an **int** store the ladder size, an **ifstream** object to open the file containing valid words, a **string** to store the user's inputted word, and a **bool** to store whether a ladder given the beginning and destination words is found. After carefully examining the skeleton, I add more detail to it. Also, inside **ladder()**, after I call **ladder()** recursively, what should I do? There are two possibilities: the ladder is found and **success** is set true; and the ladder is not found and **success** remains false. In the first case, we don't need to do anything. In the second case, however, we need to pop out the word at the back of the solution vector because that word leads to failure in locating a valid word ladder. The following updated skeleton will reflect a small modification in **ladder()**:

```
bool isValid(string, string);
void ladder(string, int, bool&);
bool isRepeated(string);
void remove(string);
bool allLetter(string);

int main(int argc, char **argv) {
- exit if no file is provided in command line

bool bitmap[26][26][26][26];
vector<string> words;          /* the solution vector */
int i, i2, i3, i4, transition;
ifstream fin;
string word;
bool success;
```

- initialize the random number generator
- open the given file and use a 4-dimensional bool array to store valid words
- prompt the user to enter a valid ladder size
- use a while loop to find a word ladder of that size given the beginning and destination words

     if found, break the while loop and start the game

     if not found, issue an error message and exit
- start the game by having the user input the intermediate words in the word ladder, given the beginning and destination words
- make sure at each stage the user enters a valid word; if not, have him or her enter again
- output results depending on how the user did
}

```
/*
precondition: first and second must consist of only letters and must be of length 4
postcondition: return true if transition from first to second is valid and second
is a word in the word list
*/
bool isValid(string first, string second) {
```
- same
```
}
```

```
/*
precondition: success should be false in the first function call
          t should be >= 1
          w must be a 4-letter string
postcondition: success is set true if the word ladder has been found
*/
void ladder(string w, int t, bool & success) {
```
- put w into the solution vector
- if t is 0, set success to true and return
- iterate from 'a' through 'z' in the first letter of w

     if the new word is a valid word and is not in the solution vector, that means this is a valid word in the ladder; call ladder recursively with this new word

     if success is false, pop out the word at the back of the solution vector
- iterate from 'a' through 'z' in the second letter of w

      if the new word is a valid word and is not in the solution vector, that means this is a valid word in the ladder; call ladder recursively with this new word

      if success is false, pop out the word at the back of the solution vector
- iterate from 'a' through 'z' in the third letter of w

      if the new word is a valid word and is not in the solution vector, that means this is a valid word in the ladder; call ladder recursively with this new word

      if success is false, pop out the word at the back of the solution vector
- iterate from 'a' through 'z' in the fourth letter of w

      if the new word is a valid word and is not in the solution vector, that means this is a valid word in the ladder; call ladder recursively with this new word

      if success is false, pop out the word at the back of the solution vector

```
}

/*
precondition: w can be any string
postcondition: return true if w is in the word list; return false otherwise
*/
bool isRepeated(string w) {
- same
}

/*
precondition: w can be any string
postcondition: remove w from the word list
*/
void remove(string w) {
- same
}

/*
precondition: w must be a 4-character string
postcondition: return true if w is alphabetic; return false otherwise
*/
bool allLetter(string w) {
- same
}
```

Step 3:

<u>Interrelation</u>: Elements of both **bitmap** and **words** can be accessed via [], so make sure their indices do not go out of their bounds. Also, pay attention to the condition of a while loop.

<u>State</u>: Let's focus on the critical variables in this program, including **bitmap** and **words**. Obviously, **bitmap** is a critical variable because it keeps track of all valid words. Once it is assigned correct values, they should never be changed. Its use solely lies in checking if a given word is valid. Therefore, we need to make sure we do nothing to alter its contents. Let's look at **words**, the solution vector. It is supposed to store all words in the word ladder, including its beginning and destination words. Once a randomly selected beginning word does not work, it should be cleared of its contents for the next attempt.

<u>Scope</u>: **bitmap** definitely merits a global scope because several functions need it. On the other hand, **ladder()** needs access to **words**, so we can make **words** global, too.

If the chosen beginning word does not lead to a valid word ladder, we should randomly select another word. But there is still a chance of selecting that word, so we should remove it from a **vector** that initially holds all words in the file, then randomly select a word in that **vector** as the beginning word. Where is this **vector**? It is not even in our skeleton! Therefore, we need one more string **vector** which assists us in making second attempts. On the other hand, inside **ladder()**, when we know that an intermediate word in the word ladder leads nowhere, we need to remember to remove that word from **words**. Without doing these, **words** is likely to contain many words, which would add to the fun of debugging later.

Step 4: Having considered step 3, I code my program efficiently because I know exactly what to do and what to be cautious about. As I code, I realize that I need slightly more variables. Here is the final version of my program:

```
/*
Michael Wen
6/19/2003
This program plays a word ladder game with the user.
*/
#include <iostream>
#include <fstream>
#include <cctype>
#include <ctime>
#include <vector>
#include <string>
```

```cpp
using namespace std;

bool bitmap[26][26][26][26];
vector<string> bitmapv, words;

bool isValid(string, string);
void ladder(string, int, bool&);
bool isRepeated(string);
void remove(string);
bool allLetter(string);

int main(int argc, char **argv) {
/* exit if no file is provided in command line */
    if(argc!=2) {
        cout << "usage: exe <wordlist>\n";
        cout << "<wordlist>: a list of words to be used in the game\n";
        exit(1);
    }

    int i, i2, i3, i4, transition, n;
    ifstream fin;
    string word, currWord;
    bool success;
/* initialize the random number generator */
    srand(time(0));
    for(i=0; i<26; ++i)
        for(i2=0; i2<26; ++i2)
            for(i3=0; i3<26; ++i3)
                for(i4=0; i4<26; ++i4)
                    bitmap[i][i2][i3][i4] = false;

/* open the given file and use a 4-dimensional bool array to store valid words
*/
    fin.open(argv[1]);
    if(!fin.is_open()) {
        cout << argv[1] << " cannot be opened, forced exit\n";
        exit(2);
    }
    while(fin>>word) {
        if(word.length()!=4 || !allLetter(word)) {
```

```
            cout << "incorrectly formatted file, forced exit\n";
            exit(3);
        }
        bitmap[word[0]-'a'][word[1]-'a'][word[2]-'a'][word[3]-'a'] = true;
        bitmapv.push_back(word);
    }
    fin.close();
/* prompt the user to enter a valid ladder size */
    cout << "Enter a ladder size (1 to 20 inclusively): ";
    while(!(cin>>transition) || transition<1 || transition>20) {
        if(!cin) {
            cin.clear();
            while(cin.get()!='\n') ;
        }
        cout << "Enter a ladder size (1 to 20 inclusively): ";
    }
    success = false;
/* use a while loop to find a word ladder of that size given the beginning and
destination words */
    while(!success) {
        words.clear();
        if(bitmapv.size()==0) {
            cout << "current word list cannot support this ladder, forced
                exit\n";
            exit(4);
        }
        word = bitmapv[rand()%bitmapv.size()];
        remove(word);
        ladder(word, transition, success);
    }


/* start the game by having the user input the intermediate words in the word
ladder, given the beginning and destination words */
    cout << "At any time, enter q to exit the game, r to restart the game,\n";
    cout << "and s to show solution.\n";
    cout << "\nEnter words from " << words.front() << " to " << words.back()
        << ":\n";
    cout << words.front() << endl;
    n = 0;
    currWord = words.front();
```

```
        while(n<transition) {
            cin >> word;
            if(word=="q") {
                break;
            }
            if(word=="r") {
                cout << "\nrestarting...";
                n = 0;
                currWord = words.front();
                cout << "done\n";
                cout << "Enter words from " << words.front() << " to ";
                cout << words.back() << ":\n";
                cout << words.front() << endl;
                continue;
            }
            if(word=="s") {
                cout << "\nhere is sample solution:\n";
                for(i=0; i<words.size(); i++)
                    cout << words[i] << endl;
                break;
            }
/* make sure at each stage the user enters a valid word */
            if(word.length()!=4 || !allLetter(word) || !isValid(currWord, word)) {
                cout << word << " is not valid. Enter a new word: ";
                continue;
            }
            currWord = word;
            ++n;
        }
/* output results depending on how the user did */
        if(currWord==words.back())
            cout << "\nCongradulations!\n";
        else
            cout << "\nI am sorry. Please try again next time.\n";
        return 0;
}

/*
precondition: first and second must consist of only letters and must be of length 4
```

```
postcondition: return true if transition from first to second is valid and second
is a word in the word list
*/
bool isValid(string first, string second) {
    int i, counter;
    counter = 0;
    if(!bitmap[second[0]-'a'][second[1]-'a'][second[2]-'a'][second[3]-'a'])
        return false;
    for(i=0; i<4; i++) {
        if(first[i]!=second[i])
            ++counter;
    }
    return (counter==1);
}


/*
precondition: success should be false in the first function call
        t should be >= 1
        w must be a 4-letter string
postcondition: success is set true if the word ladder has been found
*/
void ladder(string w, int t, bool & success) {
/* put w into the solution vector */
    words.push_back(w);
/* if t is 0, set success to true and return */
    if(t==0) {
        success = true;
        return;
    }
    string newWord = w;
    char c;
/* iterate from 'a' through 'z' in the first letter of w */
    for(c='a'; c<='z' && !success; ++c) {
        newWord[0] = c;
        if(bitmap[newWord[0]-'a'][newWord[1]-'a'][newWord[2]-
        'a'][newWord[3]-'a'] && !isRepeated(newWord)) {
            ladder(newWord, t-1, success);
            if(!success)
                words.pop_back();
        }
```

```
        }
        newWord = w;
/* iterate from 'a' through 'z' in the second letter of w */
        for(c='a'; c<='z' && !success; ++c) {
            newWord[1] = c;
            if(bitmap[newWord[0]-'a'][newWord[1]-'a'][newWord[2]-
            'a'][newWord[3]-'a'] && !isRepeated(newWord)) {
                ladder(newWord, t-1, success);
                if(!success)
                    words.pop_back();
            }
        }
        newWord = w;
/* iterate from 'a' through 'z' in the third letter of w */
        for(c='a'; c<='z' && !success; ++c) {
            newWord[2] = c;
            if(bitmap[newWord[0]-'a'][newWord[1]-'a'][newWord[2]-
            'a'][newWord[3]-'a'] && !isRepeated(newWord)) {
                ladder(newWord, t-1, success);
                if(!success)
                    words.pop_back();
            }
        }
        newWord = w;
/* iterate from 'a' through 'z' in the fourth letter of w */
        for(c='a'; c<='z' && !success; ++c) {
            newWord[3] = c;
            if(bitmap[newWord[0]-'a'][newWord[1]-'a'][newWord[2]-
            'a'][newWord[3]-'a'] && !isRepeated(newWord)) {
                ladder(newWord, t-1, success);
                if(!success)
                    words.pop_back();
            }
        }
    }
}

/*
precondition: w can be any string
postcondition: return true if w is in words; return false otherwise
*/
```

```
bool isRepeated(string w) {
    int i;
    for(i=0; i<words.size(); ++i)
        if(words[i]==w)
            return true;
    return false;
}


/*
precondition: w can be any string
postcondition: remove w from bitmapv if w exists in bitmapv
*/
void remove(string w) {
    vector<string>::iterator vi;
    for(vi=bitmapv.begin(); vi!=bitmapv.end(); ++vi)
        if(*vi==w) {
            bitmapv.erase(vi);
            break;
        }
}


/*
precondition: w must be a 4-character string
postcondition: return true if w is alphabetic; return false otherwise
*/
bool allLetter(string w) {
    return (isalpha(w[0])&&isalpha(w[1])&&isalpha(w[2])&&isalpha(w[3]));
}
```

This is a rather big program. Give yourself a big hand if you wrote it completely on your own. If you love challenges, add extra functionality such as give the user a hint along the way and play a word game of any word length.

15.5 Exercise #5: A Random Maze Generator

You probably have played mazes before, especially in your childhood. You enter at one point and exit at another. Most of the mazes you have played before were probably manually drawn. Nowadays with the advent of computers, we are able to instruct a computer to do this task for us. In this programming exercise, you are to write a random maze generator that generates a rectangular maze of size specified by the user. At the most basic level, you should have the program output relevant information about the generated maze, including each of its cells' location and which walls are knocked down. You can actually generate code for programming languages with graphics capabilities such as Java applet, OpenGL, Visual Basic, and Matlab so that they can display the maze. There are a ton of tutorials in these languages on the Internet, and all you need is a passion for learning.

Generating a maze is no small task for a new programmer. You can go sit on a couch right now and think about it and see if you can figure it out. Chances are that you come back utterly confused; that is, if you haven't turned on the TV yet. One way to do it is to utilize the notion of a set. Consider a 5-by-5 maze, which has 25 cells totally. The initial configuration of the maze should be that all walls are up, and that situation is simulated by having each cell belong to its own set. Now you find a wall at random, check to see if the cells sharing that wall belong to the same set; if so, ignore them because they are already connected with each other; if not, knock down the wall and merge them so that they are in the same set. The point is that there should be exactly one path to go from one cell to another. If you keep knocking down walls this way, at some point all cells will belong to the same set while only several walls are knocked down. Then a maze is generated and you are done. Simple, huh? You can start writing this program and show me what you are made of. If you succeed without reading any further, send me an email. I will congratulate you myself.

Basically you need a class that defines two functions: one finds you the root of a cell and the other makes two cells belong to the same set. In addition, you should define the attributes of each cell, including its parent's id, its location, and which surrounding walls are knocked down. One thing to keep in mind is that the initial parent's id of all cells should be −1, indicating that they are all roots. The two functions, to your surprise, take only one line each in my program. Here they are:

```
/*
precondition: n must be >= 0 and < s.size()
postcondition: return the root of n
*/
int find_root(int n){
    return s[n]<0 ? n : find_root(s[n]);
}

/*
```

```
precondition: root1 and root2 both must be >= 0 and < s.size()
postcondition: root1 and root2 belong to the same set
*/
void union_cell(int root1, int root2){
    s[find_root(root2)] = root1;
}
```

As you can see in the preconditions of both functions, the arguments must be greater than or equal to 0 and less than **s.size()**. If this is not true, you will most likely get a segmentation fault. In both functions, **s[n]** is the parent's id of **n**. **find_root()** simply searches recursively until **s[n]** is less than 0; **union_cell()** makes the **root** of **root2** a child of **root1**. Given these two functions, you should have no problem knocking down walls and generating a maze. After you successfully generate a maze, you should find the solution path to that maze. In a maze generated by my program, one opening is in the upper left corner and the other one lower right corner, one indicating the entrance and the other the exit. To find a solution, start at the entrance cell and choose an obstacle-free cell to go to, and go to another obstacle-free cell. This process continues until you cannot go on anymore. Then you try another valid path recursively. Yup, recursion again. You got to learn to love recursion because it's extremely powerful. Finding the solution to a maze gives you another taste in working with recursion.

Here are the proposed steps of the program:

- exit if something is missing in the command line
- generate a random rectangular maze of the specified size
- find the solution to the maze
- output relevant information about the maze
- if you know any language with graphics capabilities, generate code and have it display the maze and its solution

This program certainly takes some time, but you are strongly encouraged to do it by yourself. I still provide my skeletons and code in the following pages. If you do it all on your own, you will gain a lot of experience and your skills will improve.

The following is a list of what my program does:

- accept two files from the command line, one is where the maze without solution outputs and the other the maze with solution outputs

- generate a random rectangular maze as well as find its solution
- output appropriate Matlab code to the appropriate files

Here is a sample maze displayed using Matlab:

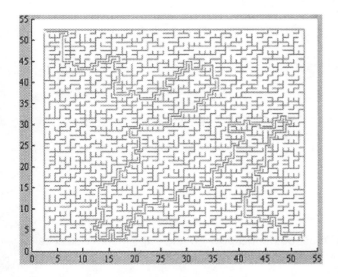

Step 1: After carefully analyzing what I need, I know I need many array data members in the class to store information regarding each cell. I use **vector** to do that because of its easy, user-friendly operations. Each cell keeps track of its right and lower walls only. For cells that do not have both walls, do something to distinct them from the rest of the cells. For example, you can set a variable so that it indicates that the cell's lower wall must be up.

This program is a lot larger than the previous ones, so while working on the skeletons, you may be confused as to what functions or class you need. You can start with **main**() and develop from there like I did.

```
void remove(int);
void findSol(int, int);
void displaySol();

class Maze{
public:
    Maze(int);
```

```
        int find_root(int);
        void union_cell(int, int);
};
/*
precondition: n must be a positive integer
postcondition: attributes of each cell are assigned values
*/
Maze::Maze(int n){
- determine each cell's location and initialize the data members
}
/*
precondition: n must be >= 0 and < the number of all cells
postcondition: return the root of n
*/
int Maze::find_root(int n){
- return the root of n
}
/*
precondition: root1 and root2 both must be >= 0 and < the number of all cells
postcondition: root1 and root2 belong to the same set
*/
void Maze::union_cell(int root1, int root2){
- make root1 and root2 belong to the same set
}

int main(int argc, char** argv){
- exit if something is missing in the command line
- exit if the user provides unacceptable information
- initialize the random number generator
- store critical data in variables
- push all elements into a vector except the last one because it has no walls
to knock down
- use a while loop to construct the maze
- inside the while loop
        randomly choose a cell
        deal with the case when the cell has 2 neighbors
        deal with the case when the cell has only 1 neighbor
- generate code for Matlab to display the maze
- find and put solution code in the solution file
}
```

```
/*
```
precondition: victim should, but not must, be an element in the vector that
holds all cells
postcondition: victim is erased from the vector
```
*/
```
void remove(int victim){
- remove victim the vector because victim is already processed
}
```
/*
```
precondition: from and to must be >= 0 and < numOfCells
postcondition: find the solution
```
*/
```
void findSol(int from, int to){
- push from to the solution vector
- mark from visited
- if from equals to, that means we've found the solution, so we call
displaySol() to write code to output files
- now go through each surrounding wall
- inside an if block

    if the right wall is down and the cell on the other side is not visited yet,
    use that cell to call findSol recursively
    if control returns here, that means this cell has led to a deadlock, so pop
    the element in the back of the solution vector

- inside an if block

    if the lower wall is down and the cell on the other side is not visited yet,
    use that cell to call findSol recursively
    if control returns here, that means this cell has led to a deadlock, so pop
    the element in the back of the solution vector

- inside an if block

    if the upper wall is down and the cell on the other side is not visited yet,
    use that cell to call findSol recursively
    if control returns here, that means this cell has led to a deadlock, so pop
    the element in the back of the solution vector

- inside an if block

    if the left wall is down and the cell on the other side is not visited yet,
    use that cell to call findSol recursively
    if control returns here, that means this cell has led to a deadlock, so pop
    the element in the back of the solution vector

}
```
/*
```

```
precondition: none
postcondition: put code for displaying the maze in file2
*/
void displaySol(){
- generate code for Matlab to display the solution to the second output file
}
```

Wow, it looks like a pretty big program. Well, it is big compared to the programming exercises you have done earlier, but it is not that big. As long as you know what to do, you will finish this program *finitely*, the sole aim of reading this book.

Step 2: As we already discussed, we need to keep track of attributes of each cell somehow. I use **vector** to store them. I need **double** to store the horizontal and vertical offsets when displaying the maze. Next, I need to store the width, height, and number of cells in **int** variables; I need to store the names of the files in **char***; I need 2 **vector**: one stores the solution to the maze and the other stores the available cells to randomly pick while knocking down walls. Finally, I probably need an **int** as an index for a loop. Given these decisions, I update my skeleton as follows:

```
void remove(int);
void findSol(int, int);
void displaySol();

class Maze{
public:
        Maze(int);
        int find_root(int);
        void union_cell(int, int);

        vector<int> s;  /* parent's id */
        vector<double> xcoord; /* right down coordinate x */
        vector<double> ycoord;  /* right down coordinate y */
/* for the next two vectors, -1 means down, 0 means must be up 1 means up */
        vector<int> down;     /* lower wall; knocked down or there */
        vector<int> right;  /* right wall; knocked down or there */
        vector<int> visited;  /* 1 means visited and 0 means not visited yet while
        finding solution */
};
/*
precondition: n must be a positive integer
```

postcondition: s, xcoord, ycoord, down, right, visited are assigned values
*/
```
Maze::Maze(int n){
- same
}
```
/*
precondition: n must be >= 0 and < s.size()
postcondition: return the root of n
*/
```
int Maze::find_root(int n){
- same
}
```
/*
precondition: root1 and root2 both must be >= 0 and < s.size()
postcondition: root1 and root2 belong to the same set
*/
```
void Maze::union_cell(int root1, int root2){
- same
}


int main(int argc, char** argv){
- exit if something is missing in the command line
        double xOffset, yOffset;
        int width, height, numOfCells, i;
        char *file, *file2;
        ofstream fout, fout2;
        vector<int> lottery, sol;
- exit if the user provides unacceptable information
- initialize the random number generator
- store critical data in variables
- push all elements into a vector except the last one because it has no walls
to knock down
- use a while loop to construct the maze
- inside the while loop
        randomly choose a cell
        deal with the case when the cell has 2 neighbors
        deal with the case when the cell has only 1 neighbor
- generate code for Matlab to display the maze
- find and put solution code in the solution file
}
```

```
/*
precondition: victim should, but not must, be an element in the vector that
holds all cells
postcondition: victim is erased from the vector
*/
void remove(int victim){
- same
}
/*
precondition: from and to must be >= 0 and < numOfCells
postcondition: find the solution
*/
void findSol(int from, int to){
- same
}
/*
precondition: none
postcondition: put code for displaying the maze in file2
*/
void displaySol(){
- same
}
```

Step 3:

Interrelation: Elements of **lottery** and **sol** can be accessed via [], so make sure their indices do not go out of bounds. Pay attention to conditions of any flow-control statements (**if, while…**).

State: **xOffset** and **yOffset** should not be changed once their values are assigned. **width, height,** and **numOfCells** are the fundamental properties of the maze and their values are not altered once assigned. **lottery** initially contains all cells' ids and decreases in size as walls are knocked down and **sol** contains the solution composed of cells' ids and increases in size as more cells on the solution path are added to it.

Scope: **xOffset** and **yOffset** are needed by **displaySol()**, so I can give them global scopes. **width, height,** and **numOfCells** are also needed by nonmember functions, especially **findSol()**. Therefore, I give them global scopes as well. **i** is just an index, so it stays local. **file, file2,** and **fout** can stay local, but **fout2** is needed by **displaySol()**. You can either make **fout2** local or global, but if you make it local, you will need to pass it to **displaySol()**. **lottery** and **sol** are both needed by several nonmember functions, so I give them global scopes.

Step 4: As I am coding, I realize I need more variables to store important information. Also, while constructing the maze, there are slightly more things I need to do than the skeleton suggests. Since I will be displaying the maze, I need to store extra information such as each cell's location. This is what **xcoord** and **ycoord** are for; they are the location of the lower right point of each cell. Anyway, the entire program is well commented, so you shouldn't have difficulty understanding any part of the program.

```cpp
/*
Michael Wen
6/1/2003
This program generates a random rectangular maze given the width and the
height.
*/
#include<iostream>
#include<fstream>
#include<string>
#include<vector>
#include<ctime>
using namespace std;

double unit=1, xOffset, yOffset;
int width, height, numOfCells;
ofstream fout2;
vector<int> lottery, sol;

void remove(int);
void findSol(int, int);
void displaySol();

class Maze{
public:
    Maze(int);
    int find_root(int);
    void union_cell(int, int);

    vector<int> s;  /* parent's id */
    vector<double> xcoord;  /* lower right coordinate x */
    vector<double> ycoord;  /* lower right coordinate y */
```

```
/* for the next two vectors, -1 means down, 0 means must be up 1 means up */
    vector<int> down;    /* lower wall; knocked down or there */
    vector<int> right;  /* right wall; knocked down or there */
    vector<int> visited;  /* 1 means visited and 0 means not visited yet while
finding solution */
};

Maze *d;

/*
precondition: n must be a positive integer
postcondition: s, xcoord, ycoord, down, right, visited are assigned values
*/
Maze::Maze(int n){
    int i,x,y,temp;

    for(i=0; i<n; i++){
        s.push_back(-1);
        x = i%width+1;
        y = height-i/width-1;
        xcoord.push_back(xOffset+x*unit);
        ycoord.push_back(yOffset+y*unit);
        temp = i>=width*(height-1) ? 0 : 1;
        down.push_back(temp);
        temp = (i+1)%width==0 ? 0 : 1;
        right.push_back(temp);
        visited.push_back(0);
    }
}
/*
precondition: n must be >= 0 and < s.size()
postcondition: return the root of n
*/
int Maze::find_root(int n){
    return s[n]<0 ? n : find_root(s[n]);
}
/*
precondition: root1 and root2 both must be >= 0 and < s.size()
postcondition: root1 and root2 belong to the same set
*/
```

```
void Maze::union_cell(int root1, int root2){
    s[find_root(root2)] = root1;
}


int main(int argc, char** argv){
/* exit if something is missing in the command line */
    if(argc!=5){
        cout << "usage: exe <width> <height> <file1> <file2>\n";
        cout << "<width>: # of columns, must be >= 2\n";
        cout << "<height>: # of rows, must be >= 2\n";
        cout << "<file1>: maze w/t solution file's name\n";
        cout << "<file2>: maze w/ solution file's name\n";
        cout << endl;
        exit(1);
    }

    char *file, *file2;
    ofstream fout;
    int i, victim, neighbor, neighbor2;
    width = atoi(argv[1]);
    height = atoi(argv[2]);
/* exit if the user provides unacceptable information */
    if(width<2 || height<2){
        cout << "unacceptable command line, forced exit\n\n";
        exit(1);
    }

/* initialize the random number generator */
    srand(time(0));

/* store critical data in variables */
    xOffset = width/20.0;
    yOffset = height/20.0;
    numOfCells = width*height;
    file = argv[3];
    file2 = argv[4];
    d = new Maze(width*height);

/* push all elements into a vector except the last one because it has no walls
to knock down */
```

```
    for(i=0; i<width*height-1; i++)
        lottery.push_back(i);
/* use a while loop to construct the maze */
    while(lottery.size()!=0){
        victim = lottery[rand()%lottery.size()];
/*victim has two neighbors*/
        if(d->down[victim]!=0 && d->right[victim]!=0){
            neighbor = victim+1;
            neighbor2 = victim+width;
/* if neither of them is joined, pick one and knock down the mutual wall */
            if(d->find_root(neighbor)!=d->find_root(victim) &&
                d->find_root(neighbor2)!=d->find_root(victim)){
                if(rand()%2==0){
                    d->union_cell(victim, neighbor);
                    d->right[victim] = -1;
                }
                else{
                    d->union_cell(victim, neighbor2);
                    d->down[victim] = -1;
                }
            }
/* if only one of them is joined, join another one and knock down the inter-
secting wall AND remove victim in vector lottery */
            else if(d->find_root(neighbor)!=d->find_root(victim)){
                d->union_cell(victim, neighbor);
                d->right[victim] = -1;
                remove(victim);
            }
            else if(d->find_root(neighbor2)!=d->find_root(victim)){
                d->union_cell(victim, neighbor2);
                d->down[victim] = -1;
                remove(victim);
            }
/* if both of them are joined, remove victim in vector lottery */
            else
                remove(victim);

        }
/*victim has one neighbor*/
        else{
```

```
/* determine which neighbor it is and if they are joined if not joined, join them
and knock down the wall if joined, do nothing */
                if((victim+1)%width==0){
                        neighbor = victim+width;
                        if(d->find_root(neighbor)!=d->find_root(victim)){
                                d->union_cell(victim, neighbor);
                                d->down[victim] = -1;
                        }
                }
                else{
                        neighbor=victim+1;
                        if(d->find_root(neighbor)!=d->find_root(victim)){
                                d->union_cell(victim, neighbor);
                                d->right[victim] = -1;
                        }
                }
                remove(victim);
        }
    }

/* generate code for matlab to display the maze */
    fout.open(file);
    fout2.open(file2);

/*first draw lines for outside walls in both files, note there are 4 openings*/
    fout << "axis([0 " << 2*xOffset+width*unit << " 0 " <<
    2*yOffset+height*unit  << "]);";
            fout << endl;
/*upper line*/
    fout << "x=[" << xOffset << ' ' << xOffset+width*unit << "];" << endl;
    fout << "y=[" << yOffset+height*unit << ' ' << yOffset+height*unit << "];"
<<        endl;
    fout << "line(x,y)" << endl;
/*left line*/
    fout << "x=[" << xOffset << ' ' << xOffset << "];" << endl;
    fout << "y=[" << yOffset+height*unit-unit << ' ' << yOffset << "];" << endl;
    fout << "line(x,y)" << endl;
/*right line*/
    fout << "x=[" << xOffset+width*unit << ' ' << xOffset+width*unit << "];" <<
            endl;
```

```
    fout << "y=[" << yOffset+height*unit << ' ' << yOffset+unit << "];" << endl;
    fout << "line(x,y)" << endl;
/*lower line*/
    fout << "x=[" << xOffset << ' ' << xOffset+width*unit << "];" << endl;
    fout << "y=[" << yOffset << ' ' << yOffset << "];" << endl;
    fout << "line(x,y)" << endl;


/*second file...*/
    fout2 << "axis([0 " << 2*xOffset+width*unit << " 0 " <<
         2*yOffset+height*unit << "]);";
fout2 << endl;
/*upper line*/
    fout2 << "x=[" << xOffset << ' ' << xOffset+width*unit << "];" << endl;
    fout2 << "y=[" << yOffset+height*unit << ' ' << yOffset+height*unit << "];"
          << endl;
    fout2 << "line(x,y)" << endl;
/*left line*/
    fout2 << "x=[" << xOffset << ' ' << xOffset << "];" << endl;
    fout2 << "y=[" << yOffset+height*unit-unit << ' ' << yOffset << "];" << endl;
    fout2 << "line(x,y)" << endl;
/*right line*/
    fout2 << "x=[" << xOffset+width*unit << ' ' << xOffset+width*unit << "];" <<
          endl;
    fout2 << "y=[" << yOffset+height*unit << ' ' << yOffset+unit << "];" <<
endl;
    fout2 << "line(x,y)" << endl;
/*lower line*/
    fout2 << "x=[" << xOffset << ' ' << xOffset+width*unit << "];" << endl;
    fout2 << "y=[" << yOffset << ' ' << yOffset << "];" << endl;
    fout2 << "line(x,y)" << endl;


/*draw interior walls in both files*/
    for(i=0; i<numOfCells; i++){
        if(d->right[i]==1 && d->down[i]==1){
            fout << "x=[" << d->xcoord[i]-unit << ' ' << d->xcoord[i] << ' ';
                fout << d->xcoord[i] << "];" << endl;
            fout << "y=[" << d->ycoord[i] << ' ' << d->ycoord[i] << ' ';
                fout << d->ycoord[i]+unit << "];" << endl;
            fout << "line(x,y)" << endl;
```

```
            fout2 << "x=[" << d->xcoord[i]-unit << ' ' << d->xcoord[i] << ' ';
                fout2 << d->xcoord[i] << "];" << endl;
            fout2 << "y=[" << d->ycoord[i] << ' ' << d->ycoord[i] << ' ';
                fout2 << d->ycoord[i]+unit << "];" << endl;
            fout2 << "line(x,y)" << endl;
        }
        else if(d->right[i]==1){
            fout << "x=[" << d->xcoord[i] << ' ' << d->xcoord[i] << "];" <<
            endl;
            fout << "y=[" << d->ycoord[i] << ' ' << d->ycoord[i]+unit << "];"
            << endl;
            fout << "line(x,y)" << endl;
            fout2 << "x=[" << d->xcoord[i] << ' ' << d->xcoord[i] << "];" <<
            endl;
            fout2 << "y=[" << d->ycoord[i] << ' ' << d->ycoord[i]+unit <<
            "];" << endl;
            fout2 << "line(x,y)" << endl;
        }
        else if(d->down[i]==1){
            fout << "x=[" << d->xcoord[i]-unit << ' ' << d->xcoord[i] << "];"
            << endl;
            fout << "y=[" << d->ycoord[i] << ' ' << d->ycoord[i] << "];" <<
            endl;
            fout << "line(x,y)" << endl;
            fout2 << "x=[" << d->xcoord[i]-unit << ' ' << d->xcoord[i] <<
            "];" << endl;
            fout2 << "y=[" << d->ycoord[i] << ' ' << d->ycoord[i] << "];" <<
            endl;
            fout2 << "line(x,y)" << endl;
        }
    }
    fout.close();

/* find and put solution code in the solution file */
    findSol(0, numOfCells-1);

    return 0;
}

/*
```

```
precondition: victim should, but not must, be an element in lottery
postcondition: victim is erased from lottery
*/
void remove(int victim){
    vector<int>::iterator vi;
    for(vi=lottery.begin(); vi!=lottery.end(); vi++)
        if(*vi==victim){
            lottery.erase(vi);
            return;
        }
}
/*
precondition: from and to must be >= 0 and < numOfCells
postcondition: findSol terminates by either calling displaySol or running out;
sol stores the solution to the maze
*/
void findSol(int from, int to){
    sol.push_back(from);
    d->visited[from] = 1;
    if(from==to){
        displaySol();
        exit(0);
    }
/*right wall is knocked down*/
    if(from>=0 && from<numOfCells && d->right[from]==-1){
        if(d->visited[from+1]!=1) {
            findSol(from+1, to);
            sol.pop_back();
        }
    }
/*lower wall is knocked down*/
    if(from>=0 && from<numOfCells && d->down[from]==-1){
        if(d->visited[from+width]!=1) {
            findSol(from+width, to);
            sol.pop_back();
        }
    }
/*upper wall is knocked down*/
    if(from-width>=1 && from-width<numOfCells &&
        d->down[from-width]==-1){
```

```
        if(d->visited[from-width]!=1) {
            findSol(from-width, to);
            sol.pop_back();
        }
    }
}
/*left wall is knocked down*/
    if(from%width!=0 && from-1>=1 && from-1<numOfCells &&
        d->right[from-1]==-1){
        if(d->visited[from-1]!=1) {
            findSol(from-1, to);
            sol.pop_back();
        }
    }
}
/*
precondition: none
postcondition: put code for displaying the maze in file2
*/
void displaySol(){
    int i;

    if(sol.size()<=1){
        fout2.close();
        return;
    }
    fout2 << "hold on\n";
/* construct vectors x and y then use plot command to plot 'g' in plot means
green */
    fout2 << "x=[";
    for(i=0; i<sol.size(); i++){
        fout2 << d->xcoord[sol[i]]-unit/2 << ' ';
    }
    fout2 << "];\ny=[";
    for(i=0; i<sol.size(); i++){
        fout2 << d->ycoord[sol[i]]+unit/2 << ' ';
    }
    fout2 << "];" << endl;
    fout2 << "plot(x,y,'g')" << endl;

    fout2.close();
```

}

If you have written the entire program by yourself, then you definitely see a marked improvement in your skills. If you are ambitious and adventurous enough, you can try writing a maze generator that generates a maze of a regular polygon of specified shape such as a triangle, a pentagon, or a hexagon. This program takes a lot of math skills, particularly in geometry, and knowing geometry well certainly gives you an edge with writing this program. This is yet another example on how closely related programming and math can be, as Section 16.12 discusses.

15.6 Exercise #6: Solving Octogram Puzzle

You probably have seen an octogram puzzle before: You are given a set of pieces of different shapes and are asked to arrange them in such a way that they fit into the given panel which is usually a square. You often have to experiment with each piece at different locations and get a solution by trial and error. When you do find a solution, you think to yourself that there aren't many solutions and you are a genius to come up with one. I thought this was true until I wrote a program to solve this puzzle. Amazingly, there are many more unique solutions than I ever thought there were!

There are only several basic ideas behind writing a program to solve this puzzle, but implementing them is a challenge. Let me start by giving you an idea how to approach this program. First you read the pieces in a file and store them somewhere. Then you find all orientations of each piece and store them somewhere, too. There will be 13 pieces and the maximum number of orientations of each piece is 8. Finally, you write a recursively function that tries all possible arrangements of the pieces until you find a solution. That's all you got to do.

Now there should be several things you are wondering about, and the first of which should be, "How do you find all orientations of each piece?" Obviously there are several subtle points about this program. So let's get on with the discussion. If you have the following piece

AAAA
A

then here is a list of its possible orientations:

```
AAAA   A          A    AA   AA   A          A    AAAA
A      A       AAAA    A    A    AAAA       A       A
       A                    A    A          A
       AA                   A    A          AA
```

There are two functions you will use to find a piece's orientations: **transpose()** and **rotate()**. **transpose()** is to change the piece to its reflection across the line y = -x; **rotate()** is to rotate the piece by 90 degrees clockwise or counterclockwise. For example, consider that you have a two-dimensional **char** array that holds the piece like:

```
piece p[5][5] = { {'A', 'A', 'A', 'A', ' '},
                  {'A', ' ', ' ', ' ', ' '},
                  {' ', ' ', ' ', ' ', ' '},
                  {' ', ' ', ' ', ' ', ' '},
                  {' ', ' ', ' ', ' ', ' '} };
```

After you transpose it, it should now become:

```
piece p[5][5] = { {'A', 'A', ' ', ' ', ' '},
                  {'A', ' ', ' ', ' ', ' '},
                  {'A', ' ', ' ', ' ', ' '},
                  {'A', ' ', ' ', ' ', ' '},
                  {' ', ' ', ' ', ' ', ' '} };
```

After you rotate it by 90 degrees counterclockwise, then it should become:

```
piece p[5][5] = { {'A', ' ', ' ', ' ', ' '},
                  {'A', 'A', 'A', 'A', ' '},
                  {' ', ' ', ' ', ' ', ' '},
                  {' ', ' ', ' ', ' ', ' '},
                  {' ', ' ', ' ', ' ', ' '} };
```

transpose() is a no brainer but **rotate()** takes some thinking and experimenting. You'd better make sure that after you rotate the piece, the first element of the array is at the leftmost uppermost tip of the piece. Otherwise, the piece above could also look like

```
piece p[5][5] = { { ' ', ' ', ' ', ' ', ' ' },
                  { ' ', ' ', ' ', ' ', ' ' },
                  { ' ', ' ', ' ', ' ', ' ' },
                  { 'A', ' ', ' ', ' ', ' ' },
                  { 'A', 'A', 'A', 'A', ' ' } };
```

And it will make things more complicated.

After you store all orientations of each piece, things become much smoother. Write a simple recursive function that tries all arrangements of pieces on a board; after you find a solution, display the board onscreen (in figure 15.2 you can see the board's size). The recursive function takes only several lines; however, without an optimization function to assist it, it will take an extremely long time. This optimization function is the key to solving this puzzle in a reasonable amount of time. If your program has a great optimization function, it can find a solution dramatically faster than if your program has a poor one. To write such a function, you basically scan the current board and see if its current layout will definitely lead nowhere. If so, stop trying to put on any more pieces. For instance, consider the following board:

Figure 15.2—a sample board with pieces

```
**********
*ABBBBCCD*
*AFFFBCCD*
*AFFE  DD*
*AEEE J D*
*AEG JJJ *
*IGGG JH *
*IG    H *
*III  HHH*
**********
```

Right between D and J, we see a hole. No matter how hard the program tries to fill the remaining holes on the board, it will lead nowhere. In this case, you should stop putting on more pieces; instead, you should move pieces so that it is at least possible for the current board to lead to a solution.

Here is the input file that contains all 13 pieces:

```
###
# #


  ##
###


   #
  ##
##


#####

####
   #

##
##

####
 #

   #
###
#

###
##

  #
###
#

###
  #
  #

###
  #
```

```
 #

 #
###
 #
```

Note that there is one line between any two pieces. Another important factor that affects the speed of your program is the order in which you put on the pieces. Your program should work with any order of pieces the program takes in. With a good optimization function, you are likely to get a solution in a timely manner regardless of the order.

My program does something extra. It keeps on finding solutions, and every time it finds one, it outputs the solution as well as the time it took to find it.

Get out some scratch paper (I used 5 sheets) and start the designing process of this program. You can't afford to lose another minute. This program is bigger than all the earlier ones, so I won't go as detailed as I did regarding how I followed the 4 steps. If you have worked through all the earlier programs with me, you will not have difficulty understanding my skeletons and comments. Here is a list of suggestions about how you should approach this program:

- Read the pieces from the file line by line by using **getline()**. You get an entire line, and then see what it contains and if it contains a single newline character, you know that you have done collecting the current piece and should start collecting the next one.

- Make sure the function that rotates a piece works perfectly. After you have **transpose()** and **rotate()**, write a small program to print out all unique orientations of a given piece. If you succeed, the rest is a breeze.

- Many pieces have 8 unique orientations, but there are pieces that have only 2 or 4 unique orientations. In that case, discard repeated ones and store only distinct ones.

- The heart of the program is the recursive function that recursively tries all possible arrangements of the pieces. As horrible as it may sound, it actually takes only several lines of code. Your job is to use loops to try all orientations of all pieces at all possible locations. No catch here.

- The second most important function is the optimization function. There are many ways to optimize the searching process, but you need to find one fast. In my program, I simply scan the entire board for unfillable holes. If that's the case, I stop going any further and look for other possibilities. Keep in mind that all pieces take 5 1-by-1 spots except the square piece, which takes 4 spots.

Step 1: I need a class to represent the pieces and a class to represent the orientations of the pieces. I also need nonmember functions to do relevant tasks such as outputting the board, initializing an array, and copying an array to another. In this program, we will be relying on two-dimensional **char** arrays because they can be used to represent the board as well as all the pieces.

In my design, both **transpose()** and **rotate90()** are **void** and the modification to the piece is done in their arguments (arrays are passed by reference); **allUnprintable()** is needed to determine whether a given line in the input file contains part of a piece; **impasse()** is the optimization function; **solve()** is the recursive function that attempts to solve the puzzle. I probably will need many more functions while coding. Anyway, here is my skeleton:

```
void outputBoard();
void init(char[numRows][numCols]);
bool allUnprintable(string s);
void setEqual(char[numRows][numCols], char[numRows][numCols]);
bool impasse(char[boardHeight][boardWidth]);
void solve(int);

class Trans {
public:
     char pattern[numRows][numCols];
     char id;
     Trans();
     Trans(char[numRows][numCols]);
     bool place(int, int);
     void clear();
};
Trans::Trans() {
- default constructor, so do nothing
}
Trans::Trans(char cc[numRows][numCols]) {
- copy the contents of cc to pattern
}
bool Trans::place(int r, int c) {
```

```
- place pattern on the board in the given location
}
void Trans::clear() {
- clear out the invoking pattern on the board
}

class Piece {
public:
    Trans *patterns[numTrans];
    int count;
    Piece();
    Piece(char[numRows][numCols]);
    void transpose(char[numRows][numCols]);
    void rotate90(char[numRows][numCols]);
};
Piece::Piece() {
- default constructor, so do nothing
}
Piece::Piece(char cc[numRows][numCols]) {
- acquire all orientations and store them in patterns
}
void Piece::transpose(char cc[numRows][numCols]) {
- transpose cc, and cc contains the new pattern
}
void Piece::rotate90(char cc[numRows][numCols]) {
- rotate cc by 90 degrees counterclockwise, and cc contains the new pattern
}

int main(int argc, char **argv) {
- quit if no input file is given in the command line
- quit if the input file is invalid
- acquire the pieces from the input file and store them in appropriate places
- declare and initialize a two-dimensional array that symbolizes the board
- solve the puzzle and outputs solutions
}

void outputBoard() {
- display the board
}
void init(char cc[numRows][numCols]) {
```

- initialize cc by making every element in the array a space
}
bool allUnprintable(string s) {
- return true if s doesn't contain '#'; return false otherwise
}
void setEqual(char cc[numRows][numCols], char cc2[numRows][numCols]) {
- set the contents of cc equal to those of cc2
}
bool impasse(char b[boardHeight][boardWidth]) {
- detect various board layouts that definitely lead nowhere to speed up the process of finding the solution
}
void solve(int n) {
- try all arrangements of the pieces recursively
}

Step 2: We need variables to store attributes of the board and the pieces, including the total number of the pieces, the maximum number of orientations of a piece, the maximum number of rows a piece occupies, the maximum number of columns a piece occupies, the width of the board, and the height of the board. I need a **clock_t** object to keep track of time; I need a **char[][]** to represent the board; I need another **char[][]** to store temporary piece; I need an **ifstream** object to open and read a file. The following is a list of variables I need:

const int numPieces = 13;
const int numTrans = 8;
const int numRows = 5;
const int numCols = 5;
const int boardWidth = 10;
const int boardHeight = 10;
clock_t start = clock();
char board[boardHeight][boardWidth];
char tempcc[numRows][numCols];
ifstream fin;

I make the attributes of the board and the pieces constants because their values shouldn't change throughout the program. In refining the skeleton, I realize that in order to not store repeated orientations, I need to be able to see if a particular orientation is already stored. I create a little structure that contains a two-dimensional array to represent an orientation of a piece. Given all this information, I add the following struct:

```
struct array {
    char acc[numRows][numCols];
};
```

And the following functions:

```
bool sameArray(array a, char cc[numRows][numCols]) {
- return true if the contents of a are identical to cc; return false otherwise
}
bool repeated(vector<array> va, char cc[numRows][numCols]) {
- return true if cc exists in va; return false otherwise
}
void arrayInit(array & ar, char cc[numRows][numCols]) {
- make the contents of ar equal to cc
}
```

Step 3:
<u>Interrelation</u>: Elements of **board** and **tempcc** can be accessed via [], so make sure their indices do not go out of bounds. Pay close attention to the conditions of flow control statements.

<u>State</u>: The attributes of the board and the pieces are constants because their values shouldn't change after initialized. **start** will be assigned a value once the program starts finding a solution, and won't be altered. The most troublesome variable is **board**. In the recursive function that attempts to solve the octogram puzzle, **board**'s contents will be constantly changed. In the event that its contents need to be altered in order for us to obtain some critical information, we can copy its contents to a temporary array and have the temporary array do that. **tempcc**, as its name suggests, is a temporary storage for a piece. One thing you should note is that you should initialize an array's contents after you declare the array; it's good practice.

<u>Scope</u>: I make the attributes of the board and the pieces global constants because their values should not change throughout the program and are needed by many functions. I am tempted to also make **start** and **board** global, but right now I am not sure yet. The remaining variables stay local for now.

Step 4: Let me show you my program before I explain any part of it:

```cpp
#include <iostream>
#include <vector>
#include <fstream>
#include <time.h>
#include <string>
using namespace std;

const int numPieces = 13;
const int numTrans = 8;
const int numRows = 5;
const int numCols = 5;
const int boardWidth = 10;
const int boardHeight = 10;

clock_t start = clock();
char board[boardHeight][boardWidth];

struct array {
    char acc[numRows][numCols];
};

void outputBoard();
void init(char[numRows][numCols]);
bool allUnprintable(string s);
void setEqual(char[numRows][numCols], char[numRows][numCols]);
bool sameArray(array, char[numRows][numCols]);
bool repeated(vector<array>, char[numRows][numCols]);
void arrayInit(array&, char[numRows][numCols]);
bool impasse(char[boardHeight][boardWidth]);
void solve(int);

class Trans {
public:
    char pattern[numRows][numCols];
    char id;
    Trans();
    Trans(char[numRows][numCols]);
    bool place(int, int);
```

```
        void clear();
};
/*
precondition: none
postcondition: default constructor
*/
Trans::Trans() {
     init(pattern);
     id = '@';
}
/*
precondition: cc should contain the pattern
postcondition: assign proper values to pattern[][] and id
*/
Trans::Trans(char cc[numRows][numCols]) {
     int r, c;
     for(r=0; r<numRows; r++)
          for(c=0; c<numCols; c++) {
               if(cc[r][c]!=' ')
                    id = cc[r][c];
               pattern[r][c] = cc[r][c];
          }
}
/*
precondition: r and c must be >= 0
postcondition: do nothing and return false if the invoking pattern doesn't fit in
the given position; place the invoking pattern in the given location and return
true if the invoking pattern fits
*/
bool Trans::place(int r, int c) {
     int rr, cc;
     for(rr=0; rr<numRows; rr++)
          for(cc=0; cc<numCols; cc++)
               if(pattern[rr][cc] != ' ')
                    if(rr+r>8 || cc+c>8 || board[rr+r][cc+c]!=' ')
                         return false;
     for(rr=0; rr<numRows; rr++)
          for(cc=0; cc<numCols; cc++)
               if(pattern[rr][cc] != ' ')
                    board[rr+r][cc+c] = pattern[rr][cc];
```

```
        return true;
}
/*
precondition: none
postcondition: clear out the spots occupied by the invoking pattern
*/
void Trans::clear() {
    int r, c, i = 0;
    for(r=boardHeight-1; r>=0; r--)
        for(c=boardWidth-1; c>=0; c--)
            if (board[r][c]==id) {
                board[r][c] = ' ';
                if(++i==numRows)
                    return;
            }
}

class Piece {
public:
    Trans *patterns[numTrans];
    int count;
    Piece();
    Piece(char[numRows][numCols]);
    void transpose(char[numRows][numCols]);
    void rotate90(char[numRows][numCols]);
};

Piece *pieces[numPieces];

/*
precondition: none
postcondition: default constructor
*/
Piece::Piece() {
    int i;
    for(i=0; i<numTrans; i++)
        patterns[i] = NULL;
    count = -1;
}
/*
```

```
precondition: cc should contain the pattern
postcondition: find and store all orientations of the pattern in Trans
*/
Piece::Piece(char cc[numRows][numCols]) {
    int i, currIndex;
    vector<array> va;
    array ar;
    va.clear();
    arrayInit(ar, cc);
    va.push_back(ar);
    patterns[0] = new Trans(cc);
    currIndex = 1;
    for(i=0; i<3; i++) {
        rotate90(cc);
        if(!repeated(va, cc)) {
            arrayInit(ar, cc);
            va.push_back(ar);
            patterns[currIndex] = new Trans(cc);

            ++currIndex;
        }
    }
    rotate90(cc);
    transpose(cc);
    if(!repeated(va, cc)) {
        arrayInit(ar, cc);
        va.push_back(ar);
        patterns[currIndex] = new Trans(cc);
        ++currIndex;
    }
    for(i=0; i<3; i++) {
        rotate90(cc);
        if(!repeated(va, cc)) {
            arrayInit(ar, cc);
            va.push_back(ar);
            patterns[currIndex] = new Trans(cc);
            ++currIndex;
        }
    }
    count = currIndex;
```

```
}
/*
precondition: cc may contain anything
postcondition: transpose the pattern in cc
*/
void Piece::transpose(char cc[numRows][numCols]) {
    char tempcc[numRows][numCols];
    int r, c;
    init(tempcc);
    for(r=0; r<numRows; r++)
        for(c=0; c<numCols; c++)
        tempcc[r][c] = cc[c][r];
    setEqual(cc, tempcc);
}
/*
precondition: cc may contain anything
postcondition: rotate the pattern in cc by 90 degrees counterclockwise
*/
void Piece::rotate90(char cc[numRows][numCols]) {
    int r, c, offset;
    bool found = false;
    char tempcc[numRows][numCols];
    offset = -1;
    for(c=numCols-1; c>=0 && !found; c--)
        for(r=numRows-1; r>=0; r--)
            if(cc[r][c]!=' ') {
                offset = numCols - c - 1;
                found = true;
                break;
            }
    if(offset==-1)
        return;
    init(tempcc);
    for(r=0; r<numRows; r++)
        for(c=0; c<numCols; c++)
            if(numCols-c-1-offset>=0 && cc[r][c]!=' ')
                tempcc[numCols-c-1-offset][r] = cc[r][c];
    setEqual(cc, tempcc);
}
int main(int argc, char **argv) {
```

```
if(argc!=2) {
    cout << "usage: <exe> <file>\n";
    cout << "<exe>: the executable of the program\n";
    cout << "<file>: the file that contains all pieces\n";
    exit(1);
}

int i, r, c;
ifstream fin;
char tempcc[numRows][numCols], letter;
string temps;
fin.open(argv[1]);
if(!fin.is_open()) {
    cout << argv[1] << " cannot be opened, forced exit\n";
    exit(2);
}
init(tempcc);
letter = 'A';
for(i=0; i<numPieces; i++) {
    r = 0;
    while(true) {
        getline(fin, temps, '\n');
        if(!fin)
            break;
        if(allUnprintable(temps))
            break;
        for (c=0; c<numCols; c++) {
            if(temps[c]=='\0')
                break;
            else if(temps[c]=='#')
                tempcc[r][c] = letter;
        }
        r++;
    }
    pieces[i] = new Piece(tempcc);
    init(tempcc);
    letter++;
}
fin.close();
for(r=0; r<boardHeight; r++)
```

```
        for (c=0; c<boardWidth; c++)
            board[r][c] = ' ';

     for(c=0; c<boardWidth; c++) {
         board[0][c] = '*';
         board[boardHeight-1][c] = '*';
   }
     for(r=1; r<boardHeight-1; r++) {
            board[r][0] = '*';
            board[r][boardWidth-1] = '*';
     }
     solve(0);
     return 0;
}


/*
precondition: none
postcondition: displays the current board onscreen
*/
void outputBoard() {
     int r, c;
     for(r=0; r<boardHeight; r++) {
            for(c=0; c<boardWidth; c++)
                 cout << board[r][c];
            cout << endl;
     }
}
/*
precondition: none
postcondition: make every element in the array a space
*/
void init(char cc[numRows][numCols]) {
     int r, c;
     for(r=0; r<numRows; r++)
         for(c=0; c<numCols; c++)
             cc[r][c] = ' ';
}
/*
precondition: none
postcondition: return true if s doesn't contain '#'; return false otherwise
```

```
*/
bool allUnprintable(string s) {
    int i;
    for(i=0; i<s.length(); i++)
        if(s[i]=='#')
            return false;
    return true;
}
/*
```

precondition: none
postcondition: set the contents of cc equal to those of cc2

```
*/
void setEqual(char cc[numRows][numCols], char cc2[numRows][numCols]) {
    int r, c;
    for(r=0; r<numRows; r++)
        for(c=0; c<numCols; c++)
            cc[r][c] = cc2[r][c];
}
/*
```

precondition: none
postcondition: return true if the contents of a are identical to cc; return false
otherwise

```
*/
bool sameArray(array a, char cc[numRows][numCols]) {
    int r, c;
    for(r=0; r<numRows; r++)
        for(c=0; c<numCols; c++)
            if(a.acc[r][c]!=cc[r][c])
                return false;
    return true;
}
/*
```

precondition: none
postcondition: return true if cc exists in va; return false otherwise

```
*/
bool repeated(vector<array> va, char cc[numRows][numCols]) {
    int i;
    for(i=0; i<va.size(); i++)
        if(sameArray(va[i], cc))
            return true;
```

```
        return false;
}
/*
precondition: none
postcondition: make the contents of ar equal to cc
*/
void arrayInit(array & ar, char cc[numRows][numCols]) {
    int r, c;
    for(r=0; r<numRows; r++)
        for(c=0; c<numCols; c++)
            ar.acc[r][c] = cc[r][c];
}
/*
precondition: boardHeight and boardWidth must both be 10
postcondition: return true if current board must lead to an impasse; return
false otherwise
*/
bool impasse(char b[boardHeight][boardWidth]) {
  for (int i = 1; i < 9; i++) {
    for (int j = 1; j < 9; j++) {
//cases where there's one unfillable pocket
        if (b[i-1][j]!=' '&&b[i][j-1]!=' '&&b[i][j+1]!=' '&&b[i+1][j]!=' ')
        if (b[i][j] == ' ')
            return true;

//cases where there's two unfillable pockets, horizontally
        if (j < 8)
        if (b[i-1][j]!=' '&&b[i-1][j+1]!=' '&&b[i][j+2]!=' '&&b[i+1][j+1]!=' '
                &&b[i+1][j]!=' '&&b[i][j-1]!=' ')
                if (b[i][j]==' '&&b[i][j+1]==' ')
                    return true;

//cases where there's three unfillable pockets, horizontally
        if (j < 7)
        if (b[i-1][j]!=' '&&b[i-1][j+1]!=' '&&b[i-1][j+2]!=' '&&b[i][j+3]!=' '
            &&b[i+1][j+2]!=' '&&b[i+1][j+1]!=' '&&b[i+1][j]!=' '&&b[i][j-1]!=' ')
            if (b[i][j]==' '&&b[i][j+1]==' '&&b[i][j+2]==' ')
                return true;

//cases where there's four unfillable pockets, horizontally
```

```cpp
            if (j < 6)
                if (b[i-1][j]!=' '&&b[i-1][j+1]!=' '&&b[i-1][j+2]!=' '&&b[i-1][j+3]!=' '
                    &&b[i][j+4]!=' '&&b[i+1][j+3]!=' '&&b[i+1][j+2]!=' '&&b[i+1][j+1]!=' '
                    &&b[i+1][j]!=' '&&b[i][j-1]!=' ')
                    if (b[i][j]==' '&&b[i][j+1]==' '&&b[i][j+2]==' '&&b[i][j+3]==' ')
                        return true;

//cases where there's two unfillable pockets, vertically
            if (i < 8)
                if (b[i-1][j]!=' '&&b[i][j+1]!=' '&&b[i+1][j+1]!=' '&&b[i+2][j]!=' '
                    &&b[i][j-1]!=' '&&b[i+1][j-1]!=' ')
                    if (b[i][j]==' '&&b[i+1][j]==' ')
                        return true;

//cases where there's three unfillable pockets, vertically
            if (i < 7)
                if (b[i-1][j]!=' '&&b[i][j+1]!=' '&&b[i+1][j+1]!=' '&&b[i+2][j+1]!=' '
                    &&b[i+3][j]!=' '&&b[i][j-1]!=' '&&b[i+1][j-1]!=' '&&b[i+2][j-1]!=' ')
                    if (b[i][j]==' '&&b[i+1][j]==' '&&b[i+2][j]==' ')
                        return true;

//cases where there's four unfillable pockets, vertically
            if (i < 6)
                if (b[i-1][j]!=' '&&b[i][j+1]!=' '&&b[i+1][j+1]!=' '&&b[i+2][j+1]!=' '
                    &&b[i+3][j+1]!=' '&&b[i+4][j]!=' '&&b[i][j-1]!=' '&&b[i+1][j-1]!=' '
                    &&b[i+2][j-1]!=' '&&b[i+3][j-1]!=' ')
                    if (b[i][j]==' '&&b[i+1][j]==' '&&b[i+2][j]==' '&&b[i+3][j]==' ')
                        return true;
        }
    }
    return false;
}
/*
precondition: n must be initially 0
postcondition: searches and displays solutions until all solutions are found
*/
void solve(int n) {
    if (n==numPieces) {
        outputBoard();
```

```
        cout << (float)(clock() - start) / CLOCKS_PER_SEC << " seconds"
        << endl;
        return;
    }
    Piece* temp = pieces[n];
    int r, c, counter;
        for (counter=0; counter<temp->count; ++counter)
            for (r=1; r<boardHeight-1; r++)
                for (c=1; c<boardWidth-1; c++)
                    if (temp->patterns[counter]->place(r, c)) {
                        if (!impasse(board))
                        solve(n+1);
                        temp->patterns[counter]->clear();
                    }
}
```

This is a rather large program, and there are several parts that need more clarifications. Some of you may understand the program completely, while some of you might understand most of it but need help with a part of it. Here is a list of questions and answers about this program that you may find helpful:

Q: Why do I have a struct and what is that for?

A: To explain this, I need you to understand that the maximum number of orientations of any piece is 8, but that doesn't mean it's always 8. Consider this piece

AAAAA

There are only 2 possible orientations of this piece, which are:

AAAAA

A
A
A
A
A

But to tell your program not to store identical orientations, you need to store previous patterns somewhere for comparisons later. I use a struct that holds a two-dimensional array. Then I push the struct's objects onto a **vector**. Other functions such as **sameArray()**, **repeated()**, and **arrayInit()** are necessary to make sure only unique orientations are stored.

*Q: Why is **board** a global variable?*

A: There are several reasons why **board** is a global variable. For starters, many functions need access to **board**, including **outputBoard()**, **Trans::place()**, **Trans::clear()**, and **solve()**. Also, at any point **board** always represents the current board layout. Even if a piece is misplaced by **Trans::place()**, it is removed by **Trans::clear()**. If you go through by hand several iterations of the recursive function, **solve()**, then you will convince yourself that keeping board global is not a bad idea.

*Q: There are default constructors in **Trans** and **Piece** but are never used. Can I remove them?*

A: Yes, definitely. Although they are not used, I included them just in case I might need them later.

*Q: What does the constructor of **Piece** do?*

A: It finds all orientations of the given piece and stores proper values into **patterns**.

*Q: Why does **impasse()** take as an argument the array that represents the board? I thought you already made **board** a global variable.*

A: Well, there are many **if** blocks inside **impasse()**, as you can see. The conditions in those **if** blocks are very long, and if the name of the array is **board** instead of **b**, the conditions will look much longer and affect readability. This may sound a little funny but it is the reason.

*Q: Can you explain what **impasse()** does? There are so many **if** blocks but I am a little confused.*

A: This is an optimization function that assists the program with finding a solution to the octogram puzzle. I scan the entire board and see if there are one, two, three, or four unfillable holes. If there are, I need to clear the last piece I placed because that piece caused the board to lead nowhere. Without this function, the program would keep on trying new pieces although the board definitely would lead to an impasse.

Q: How many unique solutions to the octogram puzzle exist?

A: I modified the program a bit so that it can accumulate solutions. I don't need to run the program nonstop; I can stop it today and run it tomorrow and it will automatically pick up where it left off. I ran this program over a couple of weeks, and I got more than 16,000 unique solutions (I also check to make sure every solution it finds is unique). If your optimization function allows you to find out the number of total possible solutions in a short period of time, then you are a truly exceptional programmer, or you've got some Peta-Herz machine from the future.

Incidentally, to make sure that every solution is unique, you need to store somewhere all solutions the program has found. Every time the program finds a new solution, it compares it with every possible orientation of each of the previous solutions. It is no small task but with strong passion for programming and the challenging octogram puzzle, you can do it.

LCD panels consume less power, produce less heat, and are more durable than their plasma counterparts. So why buy plasma panels?

CHAPTER 16

Big Traps and Tips

Sometimes some code needs to appear in order for some other code to work, but not every programmer knows why. This section is intended to help clear out some of the doubts. In addition, there are many pitfalls in programming. This section is also intended to reveal those pitfalls so that you can avoid them.

16.1   Using namespace std

Throughout this book you see many examples in which the statement, using namespace std;, is in their headers. This statement is called a *using directive*. <iostream> is recognized by only C++ programs. This header is C++ new style. Headers ending with .h are generally old style. If you use <iostream.h>, you probably do not need to include using namespace std; in the program's header. If you use <iostream>, you should include using namespace std; in the header so that the functions and other elements in <iostream> are made available to your program. In essence, it is possible that there are more than one package that supports the same function. In that case, how does a compiler know which version the function refers to? The functions, classes, and various other elements that belong to standard C++ libraries are packaged in a namespace called **std**, short for standard. This leads to the fact that, for example, **cin** is really **std::cin** and **cout** is really **std::cout**. However, if whenever you need to type **std::cin** in place of **cin**, you will be disgruntled like a pig. That is why the C++ committee decided to add the using directive as a standard feature. When you use the statement, using namespace std;, you no longer need to prefix the definitions in the **std** namespace with **std::**.

16.2   Flushing the Output Buffer

This is a very important aspect of C++'s output buffer. As discussed in Chapter 5, inserting print statements is useful in debugging but you need to make sure the output buffer is flushed so that you can see the output immediately. Let's explore how **cout** works. Whenever you use **cout** to output something, **ostream** buffers it and does not send it to the output device immediately. Only when the buffer is flushed will the output get sent to the destination. Here are several ways for a buffer to be flushed:

- The buffer is full (usually 512 bytes).
- **cout** is waiting for an input.
- **cout** receives a newline.
- **cout** receives a specific command telling it to flush.
- The current function terminates.

The reason for this behavior is to save time. For example, if the standard output is associated with a file, you don't want a program to send 1 byte 512 times while it can send 512 bytes 1 time. Try running the following program:

```
#include<iostream>
using namespace std;

int main(){
    int i;
    cout<<"begin...";
    for(i=0;i<1000000000;i++);
    cout<<"end\n";
    return 0;
}
```

When the program runs, it actually waits for a while, then outputs begin...end at the same time. This is because the buffer is not flushed before control reaches the **for** loop. You can append a newline to the first **cout** and the buffer will be flushed before the program waits. An alternative is to use the keyword **flush** as in cout<<"begin..."<<flush; to tell **cout** explicitly to flush the buffer (or use flush(cout)).

Another way to flush the buffer is when the current function terminates. In the above program, if you take out the newline at the end of the second **cout**, the buffer won't be flushed. But when program reaches the end of main, the buffer is flushed and output printed onscreen. You can write a function outside main and call it. When that function terminates, the output buffer is flushed.

Having examined the somewhat esoteric yet reasonable behavior of **cout**, you should realize that *if you want to insert print statements for debugging purposes, you need to flush the buffer in order to see the outputs immediately.*

16.3 Pointer Members inside a struct

Some are confused how a pointer is copied by using the assignment operator, so let's discuss it. Let's say you write a struct which contains an **int** and a **char***. If you use the assignment operator '=' between two instances of this struct, what will happen? Run the following program:

```
#include <iostream>
using namespace std;

struct citizen {
    int ssn;
    char *name;
};

int main(int argc, char** argv){
    citizen jerry, jesse;

    jerry.ssn = 0;
    jerry.name = "jerry";
    jesse = jerry;

    cout << jerry.ssn << ' ' << jerry.name << endl;
    cout << jesse.ssn << ' ' << jesse.name << endl;

    jerry.ssn=1;
    jerry.name="jeffrey";

    jesse.ssn = 2;
    jesse.name = "jesse";

    cout << jerry.ssn << ' ' << jerry.name << endl;
    cout << jesse.ssn << ' ' << jesse.name << endl;
}
```

The output should be as follows:

```
0 jerry
0 jerry
1 jeffrey
2 jesse
```

This simple program demonstrates an important point: when you use the assignment operator between two objects of a struct, the left operand copies the contents of all data members of the right operand. Then they become two independent objects; changing the contents of one object has no effect on the other. If, however, you use the assignment operator between two pointers, both of them point to the same address. When in doubt, write a simple program to experiment yourself. Don't take everything for granted.

16.4   Exceeding Integer Limits

As most of you know, there are limits to how big and small an integer can go. If you go beyond those limits, funny things happen. In this section we will discuss this topic.

There are basically three C++ integer types: **short**, **int**, and **long**. Standard C++ guarantees a minimum size for each of them:

- A **short** is at least 16 bits.
- An **int** is at least as big as **short**.
- A **long** is at least 32 bits and at least as big as **int**.

There is an easy way to find out the exact size of your system's integers. You can simply print symbolic constants provided by <climits> (or <limits.h> for older implementations) in a program. You can also use **sizeof** on a type to see how big it is in bytes. For example, **sizeof(int)** gives you 4 and **sizeof(short)** gives you 2 on most systems. Now that we understand that, let's turn our attention to the potential traps we could fall into if we are not careful enough. I have the following declarations:

```
int john=0;
unsigned int cheryl=0;
```

I deduct one from **john** and **cheryl** and print their values:

```
john--;
cheryl--;
cout<<"John: " <<john<<" Cheryl: "<<cheryl;
```

I got John: -1 Cheryl: 4294967295. Now I reinitialize their values:

```
john=INT_MAX;
cheryl= INT_MAX;
```

Add one to **john** and **cheryl** and print their values:

```
john++;
cheryl++;
cout<<"John: " <<john<<" Cheryl: "<<cheryl;
```

I got John: -2147483648 Cheryl: 2147483648

Your intuition probably tells you that −2147483648 is the minimum value of **int** and 4294967295 is the maximum value of **unsigned int**, and you hit the nail right on the head! **john** is an **int**, which ranges from -2147483648 to 2147483647. **cheryl** is an **unsigned int**, which ranges from 0 to 4294967295. As we can see, when you subtract one from the minimum value of **unsigned int**, you get the maximum value of **unsigned int**; when you add one to the maximum value of **int**, you get the minimum value of **int**. The overflow and underflow behavior can be depicted as a circle: if you move past the limit of a type, you get the value at the other extreme of the range.

You can also try the following code in your program:

```
cout<<INT_MAX<<endl;
cout<<INT_MAX*2<<endl; /* print out −2 */
```

Try to figure out why the output is −2. You can use a narrower analogous situation such as use 5 as the maximum value and −6 as the minimum value.

16.5 Short-circuit Evaluation

Short-circuit evaluation simply means that in a condition, control evaluates from left to right only the necessary expressions to know whether the condition is true or false. The following is a sample program:

```
#include<iostream>
using namespace std;

int main() {
    int a[3]={1,2,3};
    int b=4;
    if(b==4 || a[1000]==0)
        cout<<"Cheers, Kathy!"<<endl;
    if(!(b==3 && a[1000]==0))
        cout<<"Cheers, Sheree!"<<endl;
    return 0;
}
```

When you compile and run this program, you will see that both **if** statements are taken. The first one is taken because **b** equals 4 and no matter what a[**1000**] is, the value of the condition must be true. The second one is taken because **b==3** is false and no matter what a[**1000**] is, **&&** makes the condition false, which is made true by !. As we can see, 1000 is way over the bounds of the **int** array, but it is ignored. Now let's run the following program:

```
#include<iostream>
using namespace std;

int main() {
    int a[3]={1,2,3};
    int b=4;
    if(a[1000]==0 || b==4)
        cout<<"Greg is one of the very best"<<endl;
    if(!(a[1000]==0 && b==3))
        cout<<"and so is Ian"<<endl;
    return 0;
}
```

The two statements inside the **if** statements are reversed in order. Now the compiler sees a[1000]==0 first and needs to evaluate its truth first. Most likely this will result in a segmentation fault because a[1000] is way beyond its bounds.

As we can see, the feature of short-circuit evaluations can reduce the program's running time. Take this behavior into consideration whenever you write a condition.

16.6 cin.peek() and cin.putback()

While not being particularly useful, **cin.peek()** and **cin.putback()** accomplish something that may come in handy some day. **cin.peek()** returns the next input character without taking it out of the input stream. Here is a sample program:

```
#include<iostream>
using namespace std;

int main(){
    char c;
    while((c=cin.peek()) != '!')
        cin.get(c);
    cout << "You entered '!'. The next character is ";
    cin.get(c);
    cout << c << endl;
    return 0;
}
```

The program terminates when you enter ! somewhere and hit **enter** key. If the program terminates, it always outputs You entered '!'. The next character is ! because **cin.peek()** puts ! back to input stream for **cin.get()** to get it.

cin.putback(), as the name suggests, puts a character back to the beginning of the input stream. One thing noteworthy is that you must read a character before you use this function. Here is a sample program:

```
#include<iostream>
using namespace std;

int main(){
```

```
        char c;
        cin.get(c);
        cin.putback('c');
        cin.get(c);
        cout<<'\n'<<c<<" is the next input character.\n";
        return 0;
}
```

Enter any character you want. The program, before terminating, outputs c is the next input character. If you take out the first **cin.get(c)**, then the program will not work.

16.7 C++ Escape Sequence Codes

There are several C++ escape sequence codes, including newline, backspace, horizontal tab, vertical tab, alert, and carriage return. Many programmers are familiar with only some of them. The fact is that some C++ escape sequence codes such as vertical tab, backspace, and alert are not very useful in programming, but you still should know them. A friend of mine is a very good programmer and has been programming ever since high school. One day he asked me to help him solve a problem. He wanted user to type something onscreen, and after **enter** key was hit, he wanted cursor to go back to the beginning so that the user could overwrite what he just typed. To my surprise, he never knew that the cursor could ever go back! That is why I think you should know these sequence codes. Here is a brief description of how each one works:

- \n forms a new line so that the next character being read or outputted appears in the next line
- \b goes back one space
- \t forms a horizontal tab
- \v forms a vertical tab
- \a beeps
- \r goes back to the beginning of the current line

Some of these may not work depending on your implementations.

16.8 Alias For a Data Type

There are two ways to establish an alias for a type. One is to use **#define** and the other is to use **typedef**. For example, to make **byte** an alias for **char**, we do the following:

```
#define byte char
```

or

```
typedef char byte;
```

We can make an alias for a pointer, too. For example, if we want to make **bytePointer** an alias for **char***, we can do the following:

```
#define bytePointer char*
```

or

```
typedef char* bytePointer;
```

There is a danger in using **#define**. For example, consider the following:

```
#define bytePointer char*
bytePointer bp, bp2;
```

Preprocessor replaces **bytePointer** with **char***, converting the above declaration to be

```
char* bp, bp2;
```

Only **bp** is a pointer to **char**; **bp2** is a **char**. However, **typedef** will treat both **bp** and **bp2** as pointers to **char**.

16.9 Numbers Only

Sometimes you wish that user enter only numeric values. If a user inputs non-numeric characters, the program should reject it and prompt the user to try again. There are several ways of doing it, and one of them is to get the entire line of input and see if it is a number of not. If so continue; if not prompt the user for a number again. Here is a complete sample program:

```cpp
#include<iostream>
using namespace std;

int main() {
    double number[3], tn;
    string ts;
    int i;

    cout<<"Enter 3 numbers.\n";
    for(i=0;i<3;i++){
        cout<<"Number "<<i+1<<": ";
        getline(cin,ts);
        if(ts=="0"){
            number[i]=0;
            continue;
        }
        number[i]=atof(ts.c_str());
        while(number[i]==0){
            cout<<"Enter a number: ";
            getline(cin,ts);
            if(ts=="0"){
                number[i]=0;
                break;
            }
            number[i]=atof(ts.c_str());
        }
    }
    cout<<"You entered: ";
    for(i=0;i<3;i++)
        cout<<number[i]<<' ';
    cout<<endl;
    return 0;
}
```

This program should be pretty straightforward. I use **getline**() to get the entire line of input from standard input, and then see if it's zero or not. If so the number is determined to be zero. If not use **atof**() that <stdlib.h> provides to convert the string to a **double**. Note that **atof()** returns 0 in two cases: the string contains the value 0; the string begins with a non-numeric character. To differentiate between these two cases, I examine the string to see if it's "0". However if the string is "0.0", it will not pass the test and will be seen as non-numeric input. This is a disadvantage of using **atof()**. Also the string just needs to begin with a number for **atof()** to work. So "3.14abcdef~!@#" is converted to 3.14. These are the subtle points of handling the rejecting-non-numeric-input problem this way, but in general it does its job.

A better way is to rely on **cin**'s ability to tell good input from bad input. If you use cin>>number[i] as the **while** loop condition, then the condition is evaluated to true if user inputs a number (or a number appended by non-numeric characters); it is false if user inputs something that doesn't begin with a digit. In case of receiving a bad input, you need to use **cin.clear()** to reset input stream; without it, cin stops to read any further. Because bad input is still in the input stream, you need to get rid of it somehow. You can use **cin.get()** to read one character by one character until you get a newline, which must be the last thing the user enters. After that you can prompt the user for a new input. By solving the problem this way, "0", "0.0", "0.000" are all recognized as 0.

Of course you can find other ways to deal with this problem. This is the heart of programming—creativity. There are almost always multiple ways of doing something. Your job is to figure out a good way of doing it.

16.10 Pointer and const

Pointers are already confusing, but they could get even more complicated when they are used in conjunction with **const**. This section is intended to clear you of any doubt you may have regarding manipulating **const** pointers. Let's examine each case with examples.

Case 1: a const pointer pt that points to an int

```
int apple = 10;
int * const pt = &apple;
```

This declaration says that **pt** can point to only **apple** and nothing else. Therefore, you cannot make it point to another address later in the program. However, you can modify the value of **apple** through *pt or **apple**.

Case 2: a pointer pt that points to a const int

```
int apple = 10;
const int * pt = &apple;
```

This declaration states that **pt** points to a **const int**; so you cannot use **pt** to modify the value of **apple**. However, **apple** is not **const**, so you can change the value of **apple** by assigning a new value to **apple**. Also, **pt** can point to another address later.

Case 3: a pointer that points to an int

```
int apple = 10;
int * pt = &apple;
```

This declaration is what we normally use. You can change the value of **apple** through **apple** and *pt, and you can make **pt** point to another address later.

Case 4: a const pointer that points to an int, which is declared to be const

```
const int apple = 10;
int * const pt = &apple;
```

You should know from the first case that **pt** cannot point to another variable due to its const status. However, what about modifying the value of apple? If you think about it a little, you may figure out something incoherent is going on here. If **apple** is made **const**, its value is not supposed to change no matter what. However, it seems as if you can use **pt** to change **apple**'s value. Due to this discrepancy in the meaning of **const**, C++ forbids such assignments.

Case 5: a pointer that points to const int, which is also declared to be const

```
const int apple = 10;
const int * pt = &apple;
```

In this case, you cannot change the value of **apple** via *pt or **apple**. However, **pt** can still point to another variable later if you want it to.

Case 6: a pointer that points to int, which is declared to be const

```
const int apple = 10;
int * pt = &apple;
```

Again, if you think about it a little, you may figure out something incoherent is going on in these declarations. If **apple** is made **const**, its value is not supposed to change no matter what. However, it seems as if you can use **pt** to change **apple**'s value. Due to this discrepancy in the meaning of **const**, C++ forbids these assignments.

Having learned how to use **const** pointers, you should understand the difference between placing **const** before and after the type name. Consider the following declarations:

```
int apple = 10;
const int * const pt = &apple;
```

You should know immediately that **pt** cannot be used to modify the value of **apple** and cannot point to something else either. In this case, **apple** can be used to change its own value. Consider the following:

```
const char * const color[8] =
{
    "blue", "green", "red", "white", "black", "purple", "pink", "gray"
};
```

In this case, no strings can be changed and no pointers in the array can be made pointing to something else.

16.11 Redirection I/O

Many modern operating systems, including MS-DOS and UNIX, support redirection. You can always use this feature to pipe input from a file into a program or to store output from a program into a file. For example, let's say the executable name is **prog** which takes an **int** from the user. You can put the **int** in a file, say **input.dat**, then do the following:

```
prog < input.dat
```

Then **prog** will use the integer stored in **input.dat** to run. If later you want to store the output of **prog** into a file, say **output.dat**, you can do:

prog < input.dat > output.dat

When the program finishes executing, you can check the current directory and you will see the newly created **output.dat**. If the file was there initially, the new one may or may not overwrite it, depending on your script configuration and other factors. If you get a warning that **output.dat** exists and you are not allowed to overwrite it, try >! Instead of >.

16.12 Math Versus Programming

Every experienced programmer will soon realize that programming is closely related to mathematics. A programmer good at math programs a lot more comfortably and efficiently. There are millions of programs that demonstrate this point. Here is a simple example: the user enters a positive integer, n, and the program outputs the sum of 1, 2, 3,..., n. One way to write it is to calculate the sum the brute-force way: use a loop to add the numbers up and output that number. The bigger the number entered by the user, the longer it takes for the program to output the result. However, we can use a formula to achieve the same end. We simply calculate **(1+n)*n/2** and output the result. This is a much better way because it always takes constant time, instead of linear time, to compute the result. A sophisticated knowledge in mathematics and flexibility in programming help a programmer write efficient programs.

In fact, a lot of numerical work is done in C++ standard library. You can see many examples in C++'s math library source code, where functions like **pow**(), **cos**(), **sin**(), **log**() are implemented. The standard library also provides dozens of algorithms, presented in the **algorithm** header file. These algorithms include **sort**(), **merge**(), **replace**(), and many others, all of which use math a lot.

To conclude, building a strong background in math certainly helps you program more efficiently and creatively.

16.13 Where Are Your Eyes?

I am not kidding; when you are coding using a text editor, where are your eyes? Obviously they are looking at the computer screen, but are they focusing on the code as you type or no? In the past I used to spend so much time in debugging, and most of the errors were typos caused by the glaring oversight on my eyes' part. You see, we think we are so good that we can just type along as fast as possible without having to keep our eyes focused on what we type; then we go back and correct errors. Take this book for example. I finished it very early, but I needed to go back and forth trying to correct grammatical errors, syntax errors, etc. Why can't I just finish it once and for all? Same thing applies to coding. One day as I was coding, I purposely fixated my eyes on every letter I typed. After I was done I compiled it. To both my surprise and delight, it compiled fine. I ran it, thinking it would not give the results I wanted, but boy was I wrong. It worked exactly as it's supposed to. This is one of the biggest programming secrets I am letting you in on, and I sincerely hope you can take full advantage of it. Next time keep your eyes on it will ya? You are bound to be surprised at your efficiency and accuracy.

A balloon filled with vacuum instead of helium floats even better.

C++ Keywords

The following table displays C++ keywords, also known as reserved words, which cannot be used for any other purpose.

asm	auto	bool	break	case
catch	char	class	const	const_cast
continue	default	delete	do	double
dynamic_cast	else	enum	explicit	extern
false	float	for	friend	goto
if	inline	int	long	mutable
namespace	new	operator	private	protected
public	register	reinterpret_cast	return	short
signed	sizeof	static	static_cast	struct
switch	template	this	throw	true
try	typedef	typeid	typename	union
unsigned	using	virtual	void	volatile
wchar_t	while			

A laser can turn on and off billions of times a second. This is essentially how fiber optics laser works.

Operator Precedence

Knowing operator precedence well allows you to eliminate unnecessary brackets. Most programmers know basic operator precedence such as * and / are higher than + and -, but that's not enough. You may also want to know, for example, if == or >= comes first. Consider the following code snippet:

```
char * cstar = "susan";
char c = *++cstar;
```

The unary * and ++ have the same precedence, and the associativity is from right to left. We apply ++ first, then *. So c should be 'u'. You can find full operator precedence table at many places online or in C++ programming textbooks. When in doubt, write a simple program to test it. That way it sticks more than if you look it up somewhere. Remember, you can always use parentheses to force a certain order of evaluation.

Useful Functions

In this section we will see some very basic but useful functions that a programmer may need at any point of writing a program. As a note, some of the basic functions are already provided by standard libraries of C or C++. If you are uncertain what functions which library provides, simply do a search on the Internet. For example, if you are not sure what functions **math.h** provides, go to http://www.google.com and type **math.h** in the search field. I just did it and the first link that appears is http://www.opengroup.org/onlinepubs/007908799/xsh/math.h.html which contains all the functions provided by **math.h**.

Random Number Generator

Here is how to make a random number generator with seed being current date and time:

```
#include <ctime>  /* or <time.h> for time() */
#include <stdlib.h>  /* for srand() and rand() */
srand(time(0));  /* set up random number generator based on current time */
int random = rand() % 10;  /* from 0 to 9 inclusively */
```

rand() produces a random integer ranged from 0 to RAND_MAX, which is defined in <stdlib.h>.

Parsing a string

This function has been covered in-depth by Section 12.8, but in case you miss it, let me introduce to you this useful function again. If you have information stored in one single string, separated by a delimiter, you can write a function to parse the string and retrieve relevant data. For example, you can have the following string representing a person's bank account information, with # being the delimiter:

"0000#7/29/1971#CD#chris@yahoo.com#Amr#99999.99#"

The first substring is the person's id; the second one is the person's birthday; the third one is the person's account type; the fourth one is the person's email address; the fifth one is the person's login password; the sixth one is the person's current balance. I want to write a function that takes as arguments a string, like the one in the above example, and an index (starting at 1, not 0), specifying which substring to return. The delimiter the function uses is #. The function returns a string which is the substring specified by the index. Now you can start writing this function on your own as an exercise. Here is my version:

```cpp
#include<iostream>
using namespace std;
#include<string>  /* or <string.h> */

string parse(string s, int i) {
    string t="";
    int counter=0;
    bool start=false;

    for(int j=0;j<s.length();j++) {
        if(s[j]=='#')
            counter++;
        if(!start&&counter==i-1)
            start=true;
        if(counter==i)
            break;
        if(start&&s[j]!='#')
            t+=s[j];
    }
    return t;
}
```

However, if you know C++ string class very well, you probably know you can take advantage of some of the functions it provides such as **find()**. Here is another version of the function that utilizes C++ string functions:

```cpp
#include<iostream>
using namespace std;
#include<string>    /* or <string.h> */

string parse(string s, int i) {
```

```
    if(i<1) return "";
    int d, second, first, pos;

    pos=first=0;
    for(d=0;d<i-1;d++) {
        first=s.find('#',pos);
        if(first==string::npos)
            return "";
        pos=first+1;
    }
    second=s.find('#',pos);
    if(first==0)
        first=-1;
    return s.substr(first+1,second-first-1);
}
```

Conversion Between char* and string

Here the term "string" refers to C++ **string** class. In general, **string** is a better choice than **char*** because of easy manipulations such as appending a string to another string, extracting a string from a long string, and inserting a string into another string. However, some functions provided by C++ libraries can be called only with arguments of certain types. In this case, conversion **char*** to **string** and vice versa will come in handy.

To convert **char*** to **string**, simply use the assignment operator. To convert **string** to **const char***, simply use **c_str()** function provided by <string> or <string.h>. Here is a sample program to demonstrate both conversions:

```
#include<string>  /* or <string.h> */
int main() {
    char* c="firstString";
    string s;
    const char* c2;
    string s2="secondString";

    s=c;
    c2=s2.c_str();

    cout<<"c is "<<c<<endl;
```

```
        cout<<"s is "<<s<<endl;
        cout<<"c2 is "<<c2<<endl;
        cout<<"s2 is "<<s2<<endl;
        return 0;
}
```

Note that c2 is of type **const char***, not **char***. Conversion between **string** and **const char*** comes in handy when, for example, the program expects a string entered by user, then the program converts the **string** to **const char*** by using c_str() so that **open**() that <fstream> provides can take that argument.

If you really need to convert **string** to **char***, not **const char***, you can use the following function:

```
#include<iostream>
#include<string.h> // or <string>
char* convertStringToCharStar(string s){
        int i;
        char* tempc=new char[s.length()];

        for(i=0; i<s.length(); i++)
                tempc[i]=s[i];
        return tempc;
}
```

Show Time

Sometimes you would like to know how long a program runs. In this situation, you can certainly use the following code to achieve this purpose.

```
#include<ctime>  /* or <time.h> */

clock_t start = clock();
/* then the program runs... */
.
.
.

/* program ends here; now output how much time the program has run */
cout << (float)(clock() - start) / CLOCKS_PER_SEC << " seconds\n";
```

Pause For Some Time

Sometimes you would like your program to halt for some time. Maybe the output fills the screen and you want it to pause for ten seconds, or maybe you write a game in which the user needs to respond within a certain amount of time. In these situations, a function that pauses for some time will be necessary.

A crude function that pauses the program for some time is by using a **for** loop. Here's the sample function:

```
void pauses(){
    int pause = 1000000000;
    for(int i=0; i<pause; i++)
        ;
}
```

This function pauses for about seven seconds on my machine. The main advantage of using this approach is that it is very easy to write and to understand. The disadvantage is that you have no explicit control over how long it pauses for. The next function will be much better because you can control how long it pauses for.

```
#include<ctime>  /* or <time.h> for clock() and clock_t */
void pauses2(int sec){
    clock_t start = clock();
    while((float)(clock() - start) / CLOCKS_PER_SEC < sec)
        ;
}
```

Here is another version, but your platform must support the **sleep** system call. Also, the argument of the function call is a **string**.

```
void pauses3(string sec){
    string s = "sleep "+sec;
    system(s.c_str());
}
```

Conversion Between String and Numbers

The header <stdlib.h> provides the following functions for number conversion:

- double atof(const char *s): converts s to double
- int atoi(const char *s): converts s to int
- long atol(const char *s): converts s to long

Note that all the above functions have the common property that if the given string contains characters other than numbers, they still return some value; they don't crash. They also work with negative values. Conversions to **string** from **double**, **int**, and **long** need to be written by the programmer. The following function, **dtoa**(), converts a **double** or **int** to a string. It also works with negative values.

```
int getnod(int a){
    int t=1;
    while((a/=10)!=0)
        t++;
    return t;
}
bool allZeros(string s){
    for(int i=0; i<s.length(); i++)
        if(s[i]!='0')
            return false;
    return true;
}
string dtoa(double val){
    char *buffer;
    string bufs;
    int precision = 6;
    int decimal, sign, i;

    buffer = fcvt(val, precision, &decimal, &sign);
    bufs+=buffer;

    if(decimal<=0){
        bufs.insert(0,"0.");
        for(i=0;i>decimal;i--)
            bufs.insert(2,"0");
    }
    else{
        if(allZeros(bufs.substr(getnod((int)val))))
            bufs=bufs.substr(0,getnod((int)val));
```

```
        else
                bufs.insert(getnod((int)val),".");
    }
    if(sign==0)
            return bufs;
    return "-"+bufs;
}
```

Tokenize a String

This function is one of the most useful functions I have ever written. It accepts a string of anything, including spaces and tabs, then returns a vector that contains individual words in that string. You can include as many spaces or tabs before, after the string and even between any two words in the string. This function will ignore all the spaces and retrieve individual words. This function is useful in many ways. For example, you may want to keep track of information in the form of a string of data. Then you can use this function to retrieve individual items. Another example is that maybe you expect user to give you many data items with a space being the delimiter. Obviously human is error-prone and may enter more than 1 space between 2 data items or even enter tabs. In those situations, using this function to process those data is a good idea. By the way, this function is already covered in Section 12.9.

```
#include <vector>
/*
precondition: s contains tokens separated by unprintable characters
postcondition: returns a vector that contains all tokens of s
*/
vector<string> tokenize(string s){
        int i,j;
        vector<string> vs;
        int slen=s.length();

        j=0;
/* use a while loop to retrieve all tokens */
        while(j<slen){
/* skip all unprintable characters until a printable character is reached */
                while(!isgraph(s[j++]) && j<slen)
                        ;
                if(j>=slen) return vs;
```

```
            i=j-1;
/* take all characters until an unprintable character is reached */
        while(isgraph(s[j++]) && j<slen)
                ;
/* store it in the vector */
        if(j>=slen) j++;
        vs.push_back(s.substr(i,j-i-1));
    }
/* return the vector */
    return vs;
}
```

Output Invisible Characters:

Sometimes in debugging your program, you wish to see what a **string** or a **char** really contains but it may contain invisible characters such as newline, carriage return, and space. As an example, you are writing an HTTP client who needs to send an HTTP request to an HTTP server in order to retrieve some document. The HTTP request needs to conform to rules governing interactions between an HTTP client and an HTTP server. In such a situation, you need to make sure the request your client sends is valid. Here are some simple functions to achieve this end:

```
void examineChar(char c){
    if(c=='\n')
        cout<<"\\n";
    else if(c=='\r')
        cout<<"\\r";
    else if(c=='\b')
        cout<<"\\b";
    else if(c=='\t')
        cout<<"\\t";
    else if(c=='\a')
        cout<<"\\a";
    else if(c=='\v')
        cout<<"\\v";
    else if(c=='\0')
        cout<<"\\0";
    else
        cout<<c;
}
```

```
void examineCharStar(char *cs){
    int i;
    for(i=0;i<strlen(cs);i++)
        examineChar(cs[i]);
}

void examineString(string s){
    int i;
    if(s!="")
       for(i=0;i<s.length();i++)
            examineChar(s[i]);
}
```

Note that a string can be "" but a char cannot be ''.

Small Traps and Tips

- It is advisable to put the prototypes of all functions and classes right after the header. If you do not want to do it, you need to make sure when you scan your program from top to bottom, you do not see any reference to a function or a class not defined prior to the current point. For example, if function **A** uses function **B**, then function **A** must be placed after function **B**.

- If you declare an array of strings like "string s[100]", they all are initialized to "".

- The keyword "break" works only within a loop or **switch** statement. In the context of a loop, a "break" will exit the nearest loop no matter where the current control. For example, if you have 10 nested if statements within a **for** loop and a "break" is placed in the innermost **if** statement, when control reaches that "break", it will exit the **for** loop.

- In the condition of a flow control statement, only 0, or NULL, evaluates the condition to false. Other values, including negative integers, all evaluate the condition to true.

- A container variable (vector, queue, stack, etc) and an object of a class are passed by value implicitly, "&" can be added for it to be passed by reference.

- Omission of a semicolon can be a deadly bug, sometimes even difficult to track down. If compiler spits out a weird error, look at the line above the one it says where the error originates and see if you miss a semicolon. Incidentally, a class declaration and a structure both end with a semicolon.

- Implicit conversion takes place between an **int** and a **char**. For example, if you do **int a = 'a'** then **cout << a**, you get 97. If you do **char b = 38** then **cout << b**, you get &. In fact, a **char** represents a byte, or 8 bits.

- When you declare a pointer to **char**, always make sure it is NULL terminated.

- If you want to test whether **score** is greater than 80 and lower than 100, you do **if(score > 80 && score < 100)**. If you do **if(80 < score < 100)**, the compiler will not catch this error because it still is valid C++ syntax. However, the previous expression means **if((80 < score) < 100)**. In this case, (80<score) is either true, or 1, or false, or 0. In any case, it is less than 100. So the condition is always true.

- C++ and C both have a **goto** statement. However, using it usually is a bad idea, and you should use structured controls such as **if else, continue, break**, to control program flow.
- There are many ways to test for the end of input, and **while(cin)** is the simplest one. It coves more types of failures than other functions such as **while(!cin.eof())** and **while(!cin.fail())**.
- The <cctype> library provides many character-related functions such as determining whether a character is letter or a digit or a control character. Take advantage of that library.
- Use **close()** to close a file after you finish writing or reading it; if you don't, your program may not work correctly. Some implementation requires **clear()** before you use **close()**.

Resources

Where can you get a C/C++ compiler?

The Cygwin provides popular GNU development tools for Microsoft Windows. It simulates UNIX environment and you can use it to run C or C++ programs. You can find their download page on their main website: http://www.cygwin.com. You can also download free Dev-C compiler at http://www.bloodshed.net/.

Where can you find information about C++ standard libraries?

You can find information about the functions provided by C++ standard libraries at http://www.cplusplus.com/ref/ and many other sites developed by C++ fans.

Where can you find information about the Standard Template Library?

You can find plenty of information on the Standard Template Library at http://www.sgi.com/tech/stl/index.html and many other sites. Be advised that the Internet is an extremely dynamic world. If the above links don't work, simply do a search to find other resources.

Final Word

You have learned a lot. A conclusion you can probably draw from how to write a program efficiently is that there are no rigid rules to follow; everything is flexible. For example, small code size of a function is not necessarily good because a recursive function, while usually taking fewer lines of code, has an incredibly big time complexity than a non-recursive function. There is almost always tradeoff between two approaches, and you are the one who should decide which one better fits your requirements and the situation.

Also, based on experimentation, I have found that sometimes a hybrid approach is the best approach to solve a large-scale problem. You should be aware that no single approach is worth sticking to forever. For example, I wrote a program to find two points that has the shortest distance many points on a two-dimensional plane. The simple and obvious way to do this is to compare every single pair of points and see which one has the shortest distance. The time complexity, N being the number of points, is $\theta(N^2)$. However, I used divide-and-conquer approach and achieved $\theta(NlogN)$. I thought this approach is a lot better than total brute force, but to my surprise, brute force works better with a small set of points. It turns out that using divide-and-conquer approach until seven points, then using brute force gives the best run time.

"A little knowledge is a dangerous thing." As much cliché-sounding as it is, there is evident and time-honored truth in it. You need to acquire many tools and be selective in choosing which ones to use in a particular situation. Programmers tend to write functions on their own while overlooking what they are already provided with.

Therefore, my final word of advice to you is *"Broaden your horizons and be flexible."*

The average person has 2.6 million sweat glands in his skin.

References

1. Brain, Marshall. How Stuff Works. <http://www.howstuffworks.com>.

2. Kernighan, Brian W., and Dennis M. Ritchie. THE C PROGRAMMING LANGUAGE. New Jersey: Prentice Hall, 1988.

3. Prata, Stephen. C++ Primer Plus Third Edition. Indiana: Sams Publishing, 1998.

4. Stroustrup, Bjarne. THE C++ PROGRAMMING LANGUAGE THIRD EDITION. New Jersey: AT&T, 1997.

5. Tobler, Michael J., et al. C++ How-To. Indianan: Sams Publishing, 1999.

6. Weiss, Mark A. Data Structures & Algorithm Analysis in C++. Addison Wesley Lognman, Inc., 1999.

978-0-595-35189-3
0-595-35189-1